# THE RADICAL WOMEN MANIFESTO

## SOCIALIST FEMINIST THEORY, PROGRAM AND ORGANIZATIONAL STRUCTURE

D1292996

Red Letter Press • Seattle

Radical Women National Office: New Valencia Hall
1908 Mission Street, San Francisco, CA 94103
Phone: (415)864-1278 • Fax: (415)864-0778
E-mail: rwbayarea@yahoo.com

Red Letter Press
409 Maynard Avenue South, Suite 201, Seattle, WA 98104
Phone: (206)682-0990 • Fax: (206)682-8120
E-mail: RedLetterPress@juno.com

First Red Letter Press edition 2001
First edition published 1967 by Radical Women, Seattle, WA
Revised edition 2001
© 2001 by Radical Women. All rights reserved
Printed in the United States of America
*The Radical Women Manifesto* may be quoted freely
as long as credit is given to Radical Women.

This edition of the *Manifesto* was approved by the general
membership at Radical Women's 23rd Anniversary Conference,
February 17 - 20, 1990, Santa Monica, California, USA.

*Cover design:* Su Docekal and Helen Gilbert
*Book design:* Helen Gilbert

*Library of Congress Cataloging-in-Publication Data*
The Radical Women manifesto : socialist feminist theory, program,
and organizational structure. — Rev. ed.
    p.    cm.
  Includes bibliographical references.
  ISBN 0-932323-11-1 (pbk. : alk. paper)
    1. Radical Women — Platforms. 2. Feminism — United States.
3. Feminist theory — United States. 4. Women and socialism —
United States. 5. Minority women — United States. 6. Lesbians
— United States. I. Radical Women.
HQ1426.R327 2001
324.273'7–dc21

00-045955

# CONTENTS

# INTRODUCTION

**A**s I write this introduction, I think back to the exhilarating mass challenge that met the World Trade Organization's 1999 Seattle meeting. It was an upsurge the like of which hadn't been seen since the 1960s-era revolt against the Vietnam War. The "Battle in Seattle" against global corporate rule reverberated far beyond U.S. borders and signaled growing, revitalized ferment among young people and workers. Once again, it was cool to be young, radical, in sync with political events, and involved in changing the world!

It is to this new wave of rebels and revolutionaries that *The Radical Women Manifesto* will speak most directly, offering a cutting-edge guide for their search to build and sustain a movement for redesigning society.

Some may be surprised at that statement, since Radical Women (RW), founded in Seattle in 1967, is older than many of these young activists! But consider: out of the profusion of women's liberation groups — consciousness-raising circles, utopian collectives, and action coalitions — that spanned the political spectrum of the 1960s and early '70s, only Radical Women has kept alive the militant spirit of feminist rebellion. And Radical Women has not merely survived, but dramatically changed the political landscape.

Why have we had such an impact? Precisely by being audacious, multiracial, queer and straight, socialist feminist advocates for the overthrow of capitalism! Precisely by embracing a theory that explains why war, environmental devastation, and all forms of oppression are the order of the day under a system run for private profit. And precisely by, on the organizational front, having a democratic structure that enables us to act swiftly and decisively when it matters most.

When I first met Radical Women in 1972, the *Manifesto* took up only two mimeographed pages, yet it already encapsulated Radical Women's core beliefs on the cause of, and cure for, women's oppression. It described the origin of patriarchy in the rise of private property. And it explained that women's emancipation could only be achieved through socialism — which for its part, could only be won by a movement of the most oppressed, with women, especially women of color, playing a defining role. These were heady and subversive concepts — and they still are today!

That first *Manifesto* was like a lifeline to me, because it wove together all the diverse threads of my political awakening. I had become an anti-capitalist through my experiences in the movement against the war in Vietnam and a feminist in reaction to the sexism of my New Left "brothers." I had stood in solidarity with the race freedom struggles of Malcolm X, the Black Panther Party, the American Indian Movement, and the United Farm Workers Union. As a student at Cornell University in 1969, I joined hundreds of students, faculty and staff in supporting a courageous building occupation by Black students, which developed into an act of armed self-defense against racist white fraternity thugs and culminated in a uprising against the college administration by 10,000 students. When I worked at the Shelterhalf, an antiwar coffeehouse for soldiers in Tacoma, Washington, some of my cohorts were wrestling with their sexual identity and would soon number among the Northwest's earliest gay liberationists. Grappling with all these different issues, I and many others were rushing around in ceaseless, urgent activity but toward no coherent solution — a sure recipe for demoralization and burnout.

Sex — race — homophobia — war — imperialism — capitalism: no one I knew put all these elements together until I met Radical Women.

Radical Women not only connected these questions on paper, but in the streets as well — with chutzpah, humor, zest and *effectiveness*, no less. I joined up on the spot and gained as my reward a life filled with stimulating ideas and the satisfaction of having taken part in the panoramic events of our times. Only radical activism can provide this rich recompense, and I heartily recommend it.

## HISTORY AND ACHIEVEMENTS

*The Radical Women Manifesto* encapsulates the organization's *political theory*. You, of course, are also curious about what we have *done*. So it is my pleasure to present a whirlwind chronicle of Radical Women itself. Fasten your seat belts!

### FOUNDING MOTHERS

Radical Women emerged in Seattle, Washington from a "Free University" class on Women and Society conducted by Gloria Martin, a lifelong communist and civil rights champion. As a result of the class, Martin teamed up with Clara Fraser and Melba Windoffer (initiators of the Freedom Socialist Party) and Susan Stern (a prominent figure in the local Students for a Democratic Society) to launch Radical Women. In her book, *Socialist Feminism: The First Decade, 1966-76,* Martin writes that the new group was formed to "demonstrate that *women* could act politically, learn and teach theory, administer an organization, develop indigenous leadership, and focus movement and community attention on the sorely neglected matter of women's rights — *and that women could do this on their own.*"

Radical Women's blending of New Left student activists with feminist radicals from the "Old Left" socialist tradition stands out as highly unusual. The youth-oriented New Left, born out of the movement against the war in Vietnam, generally shunned the "orthodox" Marxist milieu and preached "don't trust anyone over 30." Though Susan Stern soon left Radical Women to join the clandestine Weather Underground, 51-year-old Martin and 44-year-old Fraser became fabulous role models and trainers for the young feminists attracted to RW. As a young woman in St. Louis, Martin had courageously participated in early anti-segregation protests. Fraser, the daughter of radical Russian Jewish immigrants, had joined the socialist movement in her early 20s. Both were independent working women, unionists and mothers. Their style was feisty, confrontational, unconventional, critical, caring, educational and funny. They thrived on debate and were aficionadas of literature, art, music, and cultures of all nations. How lucky we were to have them as mentors and friends!

Though people from several left viewpoints initially participated in Radical Women, all lost interest fairly quickly — except the Freedom Socialist Party (FSP). A long working relationship and parallel evolution of our socialist feminist programs resulted in formal *affiliation* between Radical Women and FSP in 1973. (The Freedom Socialist Party had been founded just one year before Radical Women. Its emphasis on women's liberation was one of the central reasons it split from the Socialist Workers Party.)

The association with the Freedom Socialist Party helped ensure Radical Women's survival in an ever-changing political environment. It also assisted us in becoming a national force, because everywhere the party set up a branch, its female comrades established a Radical Women chapter, too. Members of Radical Women found that the alliance with Freedom Socialist Party did not undercut our independence and autonomy, but gave us the ideological anchor and organizational support to sustain our uppity ways.

### ANTIWAR STALWARTS

From the outset, Radical Women participated heavily in the explosive anti-Vietnam War mobilization. Guerrilla theater marked its debut. At the first protest RW attended, the contingent arrived dressed as Viet Cong women — complete with guns!

Many male activists of the period believed that since women couldn't be drafted, they had no place in the movement (except for office detail and domestic/sexual services). Radical Women countered that prejudice by arguing that, while we opposed the draft, we also opposed the sexism that excluded women from it. We contended that "the second sex" would make the strongest draft *resisters*. In addition, members spoke frankly to U.S. Army GIs about how sexism, racism and the promotion of violence against women are essential to military indoctrination.

We urged adoption of a multi-issue stance that linked social struggles instead of the prevalent single-issue perspective that kept demands narrow and simplistic. We also went far beyond the opportunist slogan of "Out Now" and explicitly called for the victory of North Vietnam's socialist forces. In coalitions, we fought for democracy, a voice for Marxist viewpoints, recognition that women are among the chief victims of war, and an end to slavish devotion to the Democratic Party.

From the 1960s on, Radical Women's resistance to imperialist war has been consistent and, of necessity, unending. We have denounced U.S./UN/NATO-instigated interference, intervention and war in Chile, Nicaragua, Iran, Grenada, Panama, Somalia, Iraq and the Balkans — everywhere the lives and freedom of working women and men have been attacked for the sake of profits and rulingclass control.

### MULTI-HUED, WORKINGCLASS FEMINISM

Radical Women members worked with African American women from the anti-poverty program to initiate the abortion movement in Washington State with a historic march on the capitol in 1969. We campaigned for free abortion on demand, against forced sterilization of women of color, and for affordable, quality, 24-hour childcare. We shook up the moralizers with our battles for legalized prostitution and no-fault divorce. We fought police insensitivity to victims of rape and assault by lobbying for a Seattle city ordinance to institute a Special Commission on Crimes against Women.

In 1972, Clara Fraser, who had already represented herself in several court cases, taught a landmark women's legal self-defense class at the University of Washington. This was a survival issue during a time when women were routinely robbed of everything during divorce and child custody proceedings and often could not even find lawyers to represent them.

RW persistently pressed to form alliances and united fronts, including Action Childcare Coalition, the Feminist Co-ordinating Council (an umbrella organization made up of the whole spectrum of women's groups in Seattle), and the Coalition for Protective Legislation (a labor and feminist effort to extend female-designated workplace safeguards to men after passage of the Washington State Equal Rights Amendment).

Due to our understanding that the property system, not the male gender, was responsible for female subjugation, we rejected what was known as radical feminism, a male-bashing trend that alienated many women of color and working women. Because of this, our meeting hall was spray-painted one night with separatist put-downs such as "Radical Women Builds Men." But we never regretted choosing political principles over transient popularity.

Right from the beginning, RW differentiated itself from the liberal "ladies who lobby." While honchos in groups such as the National Organization for Women maneuvered to keep the feminist movement from "going too far," RW advanced the viewpoint that seeking "respectability" is a losing strategy — and one that sells out the women most abused by society.

Thanks to Clara Fraser's insight and intervention, we avoided another of the worst diseases of the movement: the tendency to trash its own leaders. When a group of younger members failed to defend Clara from a verbal onslaught by opponents at an antiwar meeting, she decided it was high time they learned what it means to be on the firing line. She pushed new Radical Women sisters to take on more responsibility and authority. Radical Women later adopted her essays "Woman as Leader" and "Response to 'Notes on Leadership'" as position papers.

Through confronting rampant sexism, the anarchistic tenets of the New Left, and the debilitating psychology of the feminine mystique, Radical Women sisters discovered that women have a natural talent for leadership — a gift the world desperately needs.

### RACE LIBERATIONISTS

The integration of race and sex freedom struggles has always been a hallmark of our theory and practice. RW has continuously supported the front-line role of women of color, combatted racism among feminist activists, and spoken out against sexism in people of color movements. We have also shown appreciation for others brave enough to do the same. In its early days, for example, Radical Women sent a dozen red roses to then-civil rights organizer Julian Bond after he made a breakthrough statement in favor of women's equality.

Our commitment to a feminism that speaks to the needs of women of color was cemented by the organization's character-defining first split which ensued after a fight over Radical Women's cosponsorship of a rally against police brutality spearheaded by the Black Panthers. A few Radical Women members claimed this had "nothing to do with women's liberation" and stomped out.

Rid of that baggage, Radical Women proceeded to help protect the local Black Panther Party from the kind of lethal cop attacks that decimated Black militants in other cities. When the police began massing in front of Panther headquarters one day, we activated our phone tree and called out a community defense guard. Radical Women and our supporters formed a human line that blocked the cops from entering the building. The threatened assault was thwarted.

I was among several Radical Women members arrested at construction sites as part of mass civil disobedience organized by the United Construction Workers Association (UCWA) to break the color line in the all-white building trades. We took considerable heat for calling on UCWA, a group mostly composed of Black men, to promote the entrance of women into the trades — but we won their support!

We were instrumental to the defense of heroic Chicana feminist Rosa Morales, victim of a sexist firing from her position as Chicano Studies staff-person at the University of Washington. We mobilized for Native American sovereignty and participated in the Puyallup Tribe's successful takeover of Cascadia Juvenile Center, a former Indian hospital. From New York to Los Angeles, we have demanded affirmative action, ethnic studies, justice for immigrants, and an end to police violence.

One of our most vital internal developments was the formation of the National Comrades of Color Caucus in 1981. This unique body consists of the members of color in both Radical Women and the Freedom Socialist Party. It promotes the confidence, skills and visibility of Black, Asian/Pacific Islander, Latino and Native members, and provides direction to RW and FSP on issues important to people of color. The caucus is a powerful tool for addressing and overcoming unconscious racism that can crop up within our organizations.

Because the caucus demonstrates the significance that socialist feminists place on the leadership and struggles of people of color, more women of color have been encouraged to join Radical Women and have become the majority in several branches.

### LAVENDER POWER

When the gay movement burst into flower in the early 1970s, Radical Women enthusiastically welcomed this key political development. Our lesbian members set to work to expand Marxist theory by analyzing how homophobic persecution connects to gender oppression and class exploitation.

Radical Women was instrumental in obtaining a Seattle

city ordinance providing employment and housing protections for sexual minorities. We have helped build militant lesbian/gay rights organizations and have been involved in innumerable coalitions devoted to preventing forced AIDS testing, squashing ballot-box attacks on gay rights, lobbying for state gay rights bills, and more.

In the 1980s, Radical Women sister Merle Woo, a popular college lecturer, noted writer and courageous Asian American lesbian spokesperson, triumphed against the University of California at Berkeley in two epic employment cases charging discrimination on race, sex, sexuality and political ideology.

The lesbian/gay/bisexual/transgender movement remains one of the most vibrant and active social struggles, and Radical Women is proud to be part of it.

### "GOIN' PROLETARIAN"

In 1974, RW recognized that we had made a historic transition from being a primarily student group to an organization of full-fledged workers. We had recruited a number of working women through helping to organize a strike and a union of low-paid employees (mostly female and of color) at the University of Washington. In the process, we developed the idea that later became known as "comparable worth." This goes beyond the concept of "equal pay for equal work" by insisting on equal pay for comparable work through establishment of objective measures of the "worth" of dissimilar job tasks.

Meanwhile, affirmative action gave many Radical Women members the opportunity to become trailblazers in the nontraditional trades. At Seattle's public power company, City Light, Clara Fraser crafted and implemented the country's first plan to train women as utility electricians. I was one of ten Electrical Trades Trainees (ETTs) who won our spurs in that highly successful program. However, for her efforts to defend the ETT program against management sabotage and her prominent role in a mass walkout at the utility, Clara was fired. She fought an intense, seven-year legal case that ultimately affirmed the right of free speech in the workplace and won her reinstatement at City Light.

Radical Women members naturally became union militants once in the workforce, and some have been sparkplugs for many years on county labor councils in San Francisco and Seattle. In the 1990s, getting unions on board in the crucial fight against resurgent fascism has been one of our paramount concerns.

Our theoretical understanding of the significance of women's mass entry into the House of Labor has also deepened. Not only have our numbers grown, but we are strategically placed in the rapidly growing and powerful service sector. Together with people of color and lesbians and gays, women are the overwhelming majority of workers. In a nutshell: our potential to revolutionize society is greater than ever.

### THE WORLD IS OUR BEAT

Sisterhood is global — especially for socialist feminists. Radical Women has expanded to Australia, and our international interventions have also increased.

In 1993, delegates from our Seattle, Washington and Portland, Oregon branches toured Russia and Eastern Europe to gauge the impact of the Soviet Union's breakup on women, workers, national minorities and homosexuals. By and large, the people they met were disgusted with the crumbling Stalinist bureaucracy but at the same time tremendously distrustful of capitalist restoration. RW's brand of democratic, feminist, revolutionary socialism attracted serious interest.

Radical Women has also worked diligently for the survival of the Cuban workers state. We have forged a special relationship of solidarity with the Federation of Cuban Women. In 1997, RW and the Federation cosponsored the first-ever International Feminist Brigade to Cuba. The brigade promoted global defense of the island, broadened opposition to the vicious U.S. blockade, and publicized the Cuban Revolution's inspiring gains for women, children, and people of color.

## JOIN US!

Radical Women brings vision, militancy, and an ethic of collaboration to the feminist movement, and we have been influential far beyond our size. Radical Women has moved public discourse as a whole to the left, toward attention to the needs and demands of the most excluded and harassed members of society. In so doing, the organization has magnified the strength and effectiveness of the feminist, labor, people of color and lesbian/gay/bi/transgender struggles.

I fell in love with Radical Women for its passion, boldness, imagination, intelligence and principle. All these qualities are as fresh today as they were the day I joined. Check out our *Manifesto* and, if you like what you read, connect with us in the great adventure of creating a socialist feminist future!

— MEGAN CORNISH
Seattle, Washington

# PREAMBLE

**T**he position of women around the world is as much one of second-class status today as it was in the 1950s, before the birth of the modern feminist movement.

International capitalism has proved itself incapable of providing the most elementary democratic rights for women. Instead, the system increasingly depends upon the exploitation of women for its very economic survival.

Today, women are still discriminated against in jobs and professions, education, legal status, social freedoms, political life, and family/sexual roles. We are oppressed as a sex and for our sexuality, super-exploited as workers, and triply oppressed as working women of color. And this subjugation, despite years of a mass international women's movement, is accelerating daily! Capitalism is in desperate straits and will even resort to smashing all civil liberties and ushering in fascism — the ultimate destroyer of women's rights — to protect its profits.

## WHO WE ARE

Radical Women is an international organization, founded in 1967 in the United States, where we are the oldest socialist feminist group in existence. We are women of color, Jews, and whites, workers and students, queers and straight women, the old and the young.

Radical Women is dedicated to exposing, resisting and eliminating the inequities of women's existence. To accomplish this task of insuring survival for an entire sex, we must simultaneously address ourselves to the social and material source of sexism: the capitalist form of production and distribution of products, characterized by intrinsic class, race, sex, ethnic and caste oppression. When we work for the revolutionary transformation of capitalism into a socialist society, we work for a world in which *all* people may enjoy the right of full humanity and freedom from poverty, war, racism, sexism, homophobia, anti-Semitism, and repression.

We believe that the liberation of women is indissolubly linked to the battle against all the burning injustices that define capitalism. We constitute at least half of every stratum of the exploited and are part of every struggle for freedom. We experience in life the commonality among all forms of subjugation and their shared origin — the insatiable demands of capital for profit. Thus, we cannot isolate our struggle by creating a single-issue movement that ignores the multifaceted reality of women's oppression. All oppressed groups are fighting the same enemy, and we must build a movement that can bring our separate struggles together. Unified we become strong.

Radical Women believes that the oppression of women is a political, legal and economic question of first priority. Women's political leadership is decisive to the outcome of all the separate movements, and accordingly, we are destined to play a vanguard part in the general movement for revolutionary social change.

We believe that solidarity and mutual aid of all the oppressed are necessary for the genuine liberation of any one sector: either we all are free or none of us is free. Only the unity of people of color, indigenous and ethnic minority liberation fighters, the working class, the youth resistance, the women's movement, sexual minorities, prisoners, the aged, people with disabilities, and all those tyrannized by capitalism can free us from our collective oppression. At the same time, we cannot and will not acquiesce to male chauvinism in the guise of an unreal "class unity" or "race unity" or "peace movement unity" or any other kind of "unity" that denies or tolerates the special exploitation of women workers and ignores the distinctive subjugation of women as an entire sex.

"Unity" that does not respect the different experiences and levels of oppression within society is arrogant, false and eventually self-defeating. "Unity" based on the lowest common denominator perpetuates caste differences between the privileged and unprivileged by emphasizing the demands of more fortunate workers at the expense of the greater needs of the most exploited.

"Unity" *at our expense* is merely perpetuation of women's subordination under a pretentious and hypocritical label.

## THE VANGUARD ROLE OF WOMEN

As political radicals, we anticipate and organize toward a revolutionary new world, reborn free.

As women, we anticipate and organize toward a new historical level of human relations based on equality and mutual respect.

As Radical Women, we understand and promulgate the concept that *the Woman Question is a decisive issue in the unfolding international revolution* because the exploitation of women has created a specially oppressed sex whose potential for revolt and capacity for leadership are second to none.

The current mainstream leadership of the women's movement is largely professional, middleclass and white. But the movement was founded by radicals and today its leftwing leadership is gaining strength, rising from the vast ranks of militant women from the working class, especially women of color and lesbians.

These women are doubly- and triply-exploited; they come into direct and daily conflict with bosses on the job and with racists and sexists on every level of life. They develop a keener awareness and consciousness of the triple nature of oppression — class, race and sex — than is possible for most white, nonworking, middleclass women.

The raw battle for survival in the everyday world has equipped women of color, women workers, and lesbians with a talent for discipline and respect for theory because the life of the poor woman, the working mother and the independent woman depends upon clearheadedness, self-control and organization. Accordingly, they demand these qualities in any movement that claims to be mature and realistic, and have no patience for idlers, triflers, coquettes, leeches and self-seekers within the movement. They have the least to lose and the most to gain by eliminating capitalism. They are radicalized and tempered by their actual victimization in life, not just by intellectual choice. Their experience is indispensable to a movement that must challenge the pinnacles of the bourgeois state and ultimately go so far as to seize power on behalf of all the humiliated and outcast.

It is precisely such women, who join nothing lightly but are ready to devote their lives completely when they do commit, who are destined for leadership of the entire movement. It is the historic responsibility of the movement to make an ideological connection to these women, a connection that always exists in the real world of jobs and workingclass/people of color communities, where women must fight together and, in the course of those battles, find solidarity and comradeship.

Our struggle for women's emancipation is not an easy one. The changes needed to free women from the bondage of inferior economic and social status involve a prolonged conflict, an endeavor that is met with great hostility and resistance at every step of the way. This resistance is twofold: from outside enemies as well as from within the movement, which is itself fraught with its own contradictions and inconsistencies.

Radical Women knows that the women's movement will have ups and downs, and that only a confident grasp of history, social theory, and tested organizational principles can provide the ballast to weather the storms ahead. *The Radical Women Manifesto* is our guide to achieving equilibrium amidst the chaos and corruption of the society around us, a guideline firmly grounded in women's historical past — in the beginnings of our oppression as a sex.

# THEORY

**W**omen have been indoctrinated with a mesh of lies and half-truths about our history. We have been taught that females are inferior, incompetent and second-class by nature; that we have been passive onlookers with no significant role in the advancement of humanity. Until we know our *true* history and how we were forced into subordination, we cannot know where to strike to win our freedom.

## ORIGINS OF OPPRESSION

In interpreting the source of the oppression of women, Radical Women concurs with the anthropological evidence, historical view, and socio-economic analysis formulated by Karl Marx's brilliant co-thinker, Frederick Engels. In his classic work, *The Origin of the Family, Private Property and the State*[1] (based on Lewis Henry Morgan's pioneering research on Native American society),[2] Engels demonstrates that the first division of humans into oppressed and oppressor occurred between men and women. This ancient schism resulted from replacement of communal ownership by private property, and of female-reckoned descent by patriarchy. This strikes us as the most logically consistent and historically self-evident explanation of our own past.

Engels does not ascribe the battle between the sexes to any inherent evil in one gender, but rather to the inexorable development of technology (the forces of production) and the corresponding upheavals in culture and family formations. This method of analysis is called "historical materialism."

To Engels and Marx, styles in family and sex relations are varied, historical, and transitory rather than biological, cultural, or psychological absolutes. The form of the family is determined ultimately by economics and by property relationships. The family changes accordingly throughout history as social systems replace each other.

Engels argues that the capacity for labor was the original distinction between animals and humans. In *Women's Evolution*, Evelyn Reed, a 20th century socialist and feminist anthropologist, built on Engels' work and illuminated women's role in the birth of the human race itself. "Social labor," writes Reed, "is the prime feature distinguishing humans from animals. In the beginning this was largely in the hands of the women...Woman's work was supremely creative; it created nothing less than the human species."[3] Human society began as a protective biological relationship between mother and child, and developed into a protective social relationship among mothers based on their cooperative labor.

Women's position in society stems directly from our role in social production, not from biology. In the primitive collective, women played an equal role in social production and hence shared an equal status with men. *Everyone* needed to work to insure the survival of the tribe and, consequently, each person's contribution was considered valuable to the total community. A sexual division of labor prevailed, but equal prestige was accorded to each group. Class difference did not exist. Women were in charge of the tribal encampment, and in the collective process of carrying out their domestic work, they were the creators and carriers of civilization. They invented the sciences of medicine, agriculture and architecture, and created the first poetry and government. Men generally hunted, fished and tended herds away from the camp.

Reed explains: "It was precisely through the technological advances made by women that men were finally liberated from reliance on hunting and moved to higher forms of labor."[4] Men were taught the skills of farming and numerous crafts by women.

Ancestry and the inheritance of personal possessions were reckoned in the female line. Complete democracy and egalitarian decision-making prevailed among members of the tribe. Each tribe was composed of various core groups, or gentes, organized in a matrilineal manner; that is, relations were determined by degree of closeness to the mother and sisters. This hegemony of communal female kinship groups is the (furiously disputed) matriarchy, the dawn of stable social organization among human beings. Its existence is proven by a vast body of anthropological evidence, including artifacts, ancient art and literature, the evolution of mythology, and in some tribes, the existence to this day of vestiges of a system of blood relationships based on mother-right.

The matriarchy is our highest model for egalitarian human relationships; women were respected leaders, children were raised collectively, and freedom of sexuality, including homosexuality, prevailed.

The source of women's power was in the original, gender-based division of labor. But when surpluses first developed through the introduction of domestic herds of cattle, it was the division of labor that gave rise to conflict and the subjugation of the female sex. The herds were male-tended and therefore, male-owned. As the size of the herds increased, they eventually yielded a surplus product of animals over and above the survival needs of the tribe. Barter between tribes was replaced by the exchange of products for money — and animal herds, which were mobile and exchangeable, served as the first money commodity. Through accumulating this money commodity, men came to own more and more individual, private wealth.

This differentiation of wealth allowed men to grow more powerful than women in the tribe and in the communal family. But men still could not bequeath their new riches to their own offspring. Their belongings, in the mother-right family system, went to their sisters and their sisters' children. To transfer their property to their own children, the men were impelled to overthrow the traditional order of female-reckoned inheritance. Moreover, their children's paternity had to be guaranteed to insure "correctness" of inheritance. In a protracted, convulsive struggle described by Engels as "the *world historical defeat of the female sex*,"[5] men effected a fundamental social transformation and seized power.

Primitive communism was supplanted by private property and mother-right was overthrown by father-right (patriarchy). The monogamous family unit emerged as a cruel mechanism devised for the perpetuation of private property through the mandatory sexual fidelity of the wife. A brutal system of control over women was imposed and eventually crystallized with the invention of the state to serve as the ultimate repressive authority.

Women were degraded by virtue of their new economic inferiority and dependence. They became chattel, along with domesticated animals, slaves, and children. They were privately owned, had no civil rights, and were used for breeding, sexual and domestic services. As the state emerged to protect the interests of the wealthy men who were the new ruling class, the enforced monogamy of the wife soon became codified in law. Life and death powers were assigned to husbands. And the inevitable corollaries of monogamy — prostitution and adultery — flourished. Soon, women were being bought, sold, and traded in the marketplace.

In primitive societies, the communal family and the community were synonymous. But with the victory of private property over communal property, the production of goods became divided between *social* production of commodities for the market, and *individual*, private domestic labor for the patriarchal family — the latter performed free of charge by women. This dichotomy between *public* and *private* labor is the actual economic basis of the titanic conflict between men and women.

The contradiction between private and public labor has been enormously intensified by modern industrial capitalism and by a calculated merchandising of female monogamy and the joys of housewifery. Freudianism, systematized into the mystique of "biology is destiny," provided the pseudo-scientific umbrella for the sexual sell. Women grew up denied, distorted or deranged — acculturated into a schizoid and insipid role.

Engels noted that "the lower the development of labor and...the more limited also the wealth of the society, the more the social order is found to be dominated by kinship groups."[6] As productivity under the matriarchy soars, wealth and then classes ensue with catastrophic results:

> ...the old society founded on kinship groups is broken
> up. In its place appears a new society, with its control cen-
> tered in the state...a society in which the system of the
> family is completely dominated by the system of property,
> and in which there now freely develop those class antago-
> nisms and class struggles that have hitherto formed the
> content of all written history.[7]

In the vast scale of time, institutions such as the nuclear family, private property, and the state are relatively new developments. But even a century ago, Engels concluded:

> We are now rapidly approaching a stage in the develop-
> ment of production at which the existence of classes has
> not only ceased to be a necessity, but becomes a positive
> hindrance to production. They will fall as inevitably as they
> once arose.[8]

Engels is sometimes criticized as parochial and accused of espousing a viewpoint that relates only to white Western Europe. Nothing could be further from the truth. Engels' historical and materialist method encompasses the *general*

THEORY

*contours of human development on a global scale from prehis-toric times through recorded history.* His work is replete with examples from Africa, Asia and the Americas, and the heart of his methodology is precisely his internationalism. When Marxists analyze human history, they understand that racial and national differences are not "natural" or scientifically based, but rather *social* categories that have evolved to serve particular forms of technology and economics — the "mode of production." The same basic economic laws are at work in ev-ery country.

Race, in particular, is a thoroughly unscientific category, as there are no biologically distinct races of humans. But racial prejudice is very real, having developed to justify the super-ex-ploitation of workers of color.

In countries where the form of the family differs from the bourgeois/monogamous family, or where the nature of the state and its ruling class differ from that of Western capitalism, it is be-cause the organization of production and distribution of wealth are different there. In colonized countries, among American In-dians and wherever else communal and collectivized societies endure, matriarchal family relations and democratic decision-making are strikingly evident. Variations exist, depending on the degree to which colonial powers have induced adaptation to in-ternational bourgeois mores and institutions.

Indeed, "African socialism," "American Indian communal-ism," and other pre-capitalist societies are the historical roots and theoretical models for modern socialism, which harmo-nizes the liberty, camaraderie and equality of primitive communism with an advanced technology and science. Throughout the ages, it is the women of color of these pre-private property societies who have embodied the proud and elevated position of women which was our beginning.

## WOMEN UNDER CAPITALISM

With the rule of patriarchy, the degraded position of women was intensified. Since then, states Engels, the subservience of women "has gradually been palliated and glossed over, and sometimes clothed in a milder form; but in no sense has it been abolished."[9] The sexism described by Engels has actually become sharper as monopoly capitalism has mushroomed and culminated in world domination by imperialism. The compulsion of capitalism for profit has come to completely dominate the system of the family and human relations generally, bringing class, sex and race discrimination to their most widespread, sophisticated and entrenched stage of development.

Marriage and the family under capitalism have not fundamentally changed since the beginning of Greek patriarchal monogamy. However, the isolation of the private household and the social/cultural reinforcements of women's inferior status have become more complex. Marriage is still a contract governing money relations and insuring paternity. And, as Engels said, "Within the family, [the husband] is the bourgeois and the wife represents the proletariat."[10]

The industrial revolution and the emergence of modern capitalism did engender one major advance for women: the reentry of women into the arena of social, paid commodity production. The advent of female and child labor in the 19th century involved a cataclysmic change in the economic role of women. This revolutionary change, however, was absorbed by the system and turned to the advantage of patriarchal private property and the state. A few women managed to become economically independent and many women became emancipated in their habits and attitudes. But the vast majority of working women found their job skills and advancement opportunities compromised by the unchanged, decreed female role of breeding, sexual service and private domestic labor. Women's reentry into social production simply doubled their labor and duplicated, on the job front, the discrimination against them in the home.

Women's traditional, unpaid labor is used to justify lower wages and subordinate, service jobs, such as those of maids, waitresses, laundry workers, secretaries, garment workers, nurses and prostitutes. The wife does not have the earning power of the husband and generally is expected to work as well as keep house and care for the children. So, even where formal legal and economic equality exists, says Engels, "The modern individual family is founded on the open or concealed domestic slavery of the wife, and modern society is a mass composed of these individual families as its molecules."[11]

Capitalists, indeed, have the best of two worlds. In the home, women fulfill the traditional functions of raising children, cleaning, cooking, washing, serving, and packing the husband's lunch so that he can go off to his daily wage exploitation. The wife's labor is extracted at *no expense to the system* whatsoever. In addition, *precisely because* women perform this mass of domestic labor for free, they are considered as slave or cheap labor and similarly underpaid and exploited as workers in social production.

It is clear that the capitalist system cannot function without the institution of the patriarchal nuclear family. The cost to capitalism of equitably paying for both women's domestic labor and our underpaid work in public industry would render profit-making impossible.

Yet, the contemporary family is collapsing. The majority of marriages end in divorce in the United States, Australia and other advanced capitalist countries. Millions of children are alienated from their parents. Ever-growing numbers of single mothers, among the lowest-paid workers, must individually bear responsibility for society's children. The disintegration of the nuclear family is generally blamed on "irresponsible females" — particularly if the mother is a person of color — or on rebellious youth, or both. But the real reason, the *materialist* root of the phenomenon, is the domination of property relations over human needs, resulting in totalitarian power relations within the family.

The nuclear family is an *economic* unit, the cell-form of the highly developed class structure of the total society: the man is the boss over the woman, crudely or subtly, and both parents dominate the children. All are forced to live together so that property can be acquired and transmitted in a capitalist fashion and so the ruling class can have its current and future workers reproduced, fed and cared for by women's free labor.

As in the larger arena of social production, the class struggle is bound to erupt on the domestic scene within the heart of the family itself. The oppressed members of the family grow increasingly alienated or hostile and finally erupt and depart. Youth rebellion, the sexual revolution, and the feminist and lesbian/gay/bisexual/transgender movements are all products, in part, of the disintegration of the family and the struggle to find alternatives to the nuclear family structure.

The contemporary nuclear family is not only reactionary, unfair and artificial; it is antisocial. It isolates women from the community and from each other. As a *private* detached institution, it breeds an antisocial individualism and nonintervention into public affairs for both parents and children. The family is the primary source of support for most people, especially among the oppressed, yet it consistently fails them. Domestic violence and the physical and sexual abuse of children are chilling legacies of the patriarchal family.

Workingclass families have always been far more fluid, far less cemented under capitalism than middleclass families. Among the working class and the poor in general, no significant property is accumulated, so no material basis exists for enforcement of inheritance laws. When the wife also works outside the home, as most women must to survive under modern capitalism, male supremacy tends to wither. A woman who can support herself has far greater freedom to choose her sexual partners and lifestyle.

Today, in advanced capitalist countries, the traditional nuclear family recedes farther and farther from reality. In the U.S., for example, only 9.4% of all multi-person households fit the traditional employed-father/unemployed-mother-at-home pattern.[12] Engels foresaw this disintegration of the nuclear family among the proletariat. "Now that large-scale industry has taken the wife out of the home onto the labor market and into the factory," he wrote, "and made her often the breadwinner of the family, no basis for any kind of male supremacy is left in the proletarian household, except, perhaps for something of the brutality toward women that has spread since the introduction of monogamy."[13]

In *Capital*, Marx added:

> However terrible and disgusting the dissolution, under the capitalist system, of the old family ties may appear, nevertheless, modern industry, by assigning as it does an important part in the process of production, outside the domestic sphere, to women, to young persons, and to children of both sexes, creates a new economic foundation for a higher form of the family and of the relations between sexes... Moreover, it is obvious that the fact of the collective working group being composed of individuals of both the sexes and all ages, must necessarily, under suitable conditions, become a source of humane development; although in its spontaneously developed, brutal, capitalistic form, where the laborer exists for the process of production, and not the process of production for the laborer, that fact is a pestiferous source of corruption and slavery.[14]

Engels concludes his analysis of capitalism:

> The peculiar character of the supremacy of the husband over the wife in the modern family, the necessity of creating real social equality between them and the way to do it, will only be seen in the clear light of day when both possess legally complete equality of rights. Then it will be plain that the *first condition for the liberation of the wife is to bring the whole female sex back into public industry* and that this in turn demands that the characteristic of the monogamous family as the economic unit of society be abolished.[15]

Capitalism destroys the nuclear family and at the same time cannot tolerate its destruction. As long as capitalist property relations survive, every societal institution will continue to hammer at personal relationships, to force them into the disintegrating monogamous family mold. Full freedom in human relations will only develop when the choice of sexual partners and living situations is stripped of all economic coercion, when capitalism and all its economic and social baggage are obliterated.

## RACE AND GENDER IN THE UNITED STATES

Through imperialism, patriarchal capitalism has made the oppression of women international. Yet nowhere in the world are the contradictions more acute between what is humane and what is economically dictated than in the United States, because it is there that capitalism is most technologically advanced *and* most dependent on the cheap labor of women and people of color to sustain its profits.

The United States has arrived at its position as supreme power of the capitalist world by a historically unique combination of economic developments. Just as the subjugation of women was the essential element in the development of the private property system and its expansion into capitalism and then imperialism, so it was the brutal massacre of the Native Americans and the institution of Black slavery that enabled U.S. capitalism to outstrip the rest of the world in the accumulation of land, capital, technology and productive power. Asians, Chicanos and Mexicanos have similarly suffered super-exploitation as cheap labor to build the West and Southwest, making it possible for the United States to rapidly become the world's foremost imperialist power.

Slavery, like the monogamous family, was fundamentally an economic institution, which prevailed until it became a hindrance to production and industrial development. Without those 200 years of legal slavery and the century of African American exploitation following emancipation, and without the ever-expanding abuse of women's labor, the United States never would have achieved its superpower status. We must never forget that both American Indian society and the bulk of the African societies from which slaves were lured, kidnapped or captured were tribal or confederate matrilineal nations that were communal in their social structure. It was this heritage that white Americans — Yankee and Southerner alike — corrupted and smashed in their mania for land, cheap labor and profits.

The African American family was ripped apart. The Native American family was poisoned by venereal disease and alcohol. And the women of both peoples were systematically degraded and crushed to the social level of virtual untouchables — the lowest of the low. Genocide against entire peoples and venal sadism against the female sex constitute the true story of American "civilization."

Capitalism has created many additional forms of discrimination to bolster its profits. Age is used as an excuse to pay lower wages or throw people out of the workforce altogether. Fewer than half of those with disabilities are employed, often at less than minimum wage, despite the fact that most become disabled as a result of unsafe working conditions, poverty or imperialist war. Gays, lesbians, and transgendered people are discriminated against in hiring, pay, promotion and benefits and are blacklisted from certain occupations.

People of color, women, lesbians, gays, the disabled, the old and the young comprise a pool of cheap labor — a reserve army of workers pulled into and squeezed out of the labor market as economic necessity dictates, a phenomenon which makes the super-profits of a few white men possible. For women of color, this has meant *triple* exploitation: as workers, as ethnic minorities, and as women.

Racism, sexism and the heritage of slavery have spawned a deep-rooted stereotype of people of color and women which is used to "justify" our second-class status. We are depicted as dependent, incapable of reasoned thought, sneaky, too emotional or emotionless, childlike, cheerfully content, and devoid of any ambition for improving our lot. Here again, women of color are doubly victimized as ethnic minorities and as women, and portrayed as biologically inferior on both counts. Women of color suffer both sexual and racial servitude in their relations with white male America.

In its insatiable lust for expanding profits, U.S. capitalism not only degrades and dehumanizes women by the stereotypes it fosters, but proceeds to profit from the stereotypes themselves. It is stock in trade to exploit women's bodies to sell everything from toothpaste to computers. This pervasive use of women as sex objects not only reinforces the artificial, vapid and alluring image of white women, but invents a grossly false standard of beauty which further insults women of other ethnic groups. The phony image of the lesbian as the sexually frustrated, sick and embittered man-hater has been used to split the feminist movement apart. And the Stepin Fetchit[16] image of African Americans fostered by the entertainment industry perpetuates racial discrimination and prevents Blacks and whites from merging forces and working together against their common exploiters.

Race and sex discrimination within capitalist society sabotage the workingclass fight against wage exploitation by fostering internal racism and sexism as well as constant competition for dwindling jobs and status. Furthermore, the ethnic freedom movements are divided by sexism and homophobia, and some segments of the women's movement harbor racist attitudes as well as the dregs of sexism in their attitudes towards lesbians and their own women leaders.

However, these deep divisions in the working class can be bridged. Women workers, particularly women of color, link sex and race consciousness with general labor issues, and are creating dynamic, militant alliances of workers. Just as we predicted in the 1960s, there is widespread acceptance of multi-issue politics today, and a growing leadership of women of color, lesbians, and working women in all the movements for social change.

In principled, multi-issue unity there is strength. Only a firm grasp of this theoretical and practical truth will provide the mechanism for lasting solidarity and victory. And it is women workers who are mandated by our unique socio-economic position to serve as the vanguard battalion in forging this solidarity. We will lead because we must and because nobody needs fundamental social change as much as we, women of all races and sexual orientations, need it to survive.

## REFORM OR REVOLUTION

The origin and depth of our oppression as women implies the solution. In the subjugation sweepstakes, we win. We are the oldest, the largest, and the most international group of persistently oppressed human beings. Only titanic social upheaval with a revolutionary scope unprecedented in human history can turn the imperialist male supremacist system upside down, restore economic equality, and then begin to reconstruct the contours of sexual politics after 5,000 years of distortion and counterrevolution.

Sexism is not simply a cancerous growth within the capitalist body. It *is* the body: sexism defines, motivates and energizes it. The roots of sexism, the arena for sexism, and the continuous need for sexism all lie in the confines of capitalism. The mandate for revolutionary feminists is to transform the birthplace of sexism — the private property system — into its opposite and only enemy — socialism, the graveyard of sexism. The bourgeois father of male supremacy must be overthrown and replaced by the matriarchal democracy of socialist economics and a humane culture.

For people of color, whose exploitation has been another central and distinctive feature of capitalism, overthrowing the profit system is logically in order. And for women of all races and sexual orientations, the intrinsic connection between sexism and capitalism should be unmistakable. The origins of oppression go back through history to the beginnings of private property and the profound division between private, domestic, unpaid labor and social, paid labor. Therefore, real equality for women demands not only the death of capitalism and all systems of private property, but the corresponding eradication of the state-enforced bourgeois monogamous family, the mechanism that perpetuates oppression.

Our freedom can be achieved only under a communally organized, democratic, cooperative society where goods and services will once again be collectivized, that is, produced and owned by all and allocated for common human use rather than for individual profit. Private ownership of industrial plants and products, and the political power this engenders, must go. The absurd conflict between the "individual" and "society" will then vanish, because they will actually be interdependent. Children of all races and both sexes will grow up sharing all that the earth and human talent can provide, free from poverty, war, exploitation, brutality and repression.

This kind of world has a name: socialism. It is realizable only on an international scale, and this global victory of socialism can only be consolidated once the revolution has been won in advanced capitalist countries. Because of the crucial role of the United States in the world economy and its giant-sized technology, revolution in the U.S. is the key to lasting fundamental change anywhere else in the world.

U.S. capitalism is, in reality, international; it stretches around the globe to steal land and resources and exploit women and Third World people. For this reason, revolution in "the belly of the beast" is decisive to the outcome of freedom struggles waged by oppressed people everywhere. Every revolution on the planet and each battle for national liberation will founder so long as U.S. imperialism has the power to co-opt, starve or bomb it out of existence. Socialist revolution in the heartland of world imperialist counterrevolution will provide the ultimate guarantee for freedom worldwide.

Despite the basic and obvious connection between sexism and capitalism, many feminist spokespeople claim that in the near future, it will be possible to *eliminate* sexist malpractices within the system through *reforms* — thus, rendering revolutionary politics irrelevant.

We believe they are simply and catastrophically wrong.

They ignore the origins of our subjugation, preferring to consider male supremacy an accidental vestige of past culture that will simply evaporate when faced with their righteous indignation, legislative pressure, legal reform and "reasonable" demands. Their view that equality for women has only just now become possible because of advances in technology that have made physical size and strength largely unimportant is, in effect, an admission that women were incapable of functioning on an equal basis before the advent of modern technology. This is anthropological nonsense.

These diehard adherents to reforming capitalism refuse to seriously dissect the causes of sexism because the result of their analysis would gravitate them towards radical politics. As professionals or women who have the luxury to retreat into the home or potential "success," these women fear and loathe radicalism and loss of respectability far more than they hate sexism. They dare not jeopardize their status, incomes and prospects.

Organizing to win reforms on survival issues is vital, but attempting to corral insurgent women inside capitalist parties, such as the Democratic Party in the U.S. or its equivalent in other countries, can only frustrate, confuse and demoralize the movement. Such degeneration ensued when feminists of the early 1900s turned to suffrage as the cure-all for female oppression. It is absurd and self-defeating to promise women full equality through the good graces of mainstream parties whose survival depends precisely on the capitalist class and its exploitation of women on every level of life.

*When will we ever stop loving our masters and joining our enemies?*

As the feminist movement has polarized into right and left tendencies, the bureaucratic leaders of the liberal feminist wing have become calculating apologists for the system and outright enemies of women's interests. Fearing radicalism more than reaction, they run from or try to make deals with the right wing, including anti-abortionists, emboldening these treacherous foes of women. Devotees of reformist politics viciously redbait and witch-hunt Radical Women because of our socialist ideology, militant stance, and often relatively unconventional lifestyles. They unabashedly censor and sell out women of color, open lesbians, and women workers to protect their "credibility" and respectability in political establishment circles.

They attempt to channel all mass protest against attacks on women into purely legislative action and capitalist party politics, thereby dissipating the power of the struggle. These reformist misleaders, many of whom gained jobs and political positions off the back of the movement, serve only one purpose — to hold back increasingly militant rank-and-file feminists through their racist, anti-gay, anti-labor, opportunism.

Other sectors of the women's movement simply reject politics, *all* politics, as corrupt, "male-dominated" and a deviation from "pure" feminism. To seek power, they say, is only to imitate men's quest for power, and women must somehow maintain the moral purity that our own powerlessness has supposedly inculcated in us. Or they reject all political struggle against our oppressors, arguing that spiritual or erotic "empowerment" is all that's needed.

To them we assert that the question of *power* — power over our own lives and political and economic power in society — is the *central* issue of women's liberation. To ignore this is tantamount to refusing to struggle against what oppresses us, which is exactly what our oppressors would like us to do.

Power in itself is not evil. The problem is its centralization in the hands of a wealthy few who use it to exploit the rest of us. The only solution is to wrest control away from them by building a mass revolutionary movement capable of seizing power and giving it back to the broad masses of working people.

There is another trend of feminists who agree with radicals that socialism is, or *should be*, preferable to capitalism, but who are sincerely skeptical about the probability of achieving it. They see the quest for socialism as utopian and prefer to spend their energies on more short-range goals. But reforms are few and far between and achieved only after Herculean effort. Even when a reform is won, the achievement will only degenerate and create a host of new abuses in its wake if the reform movement itself does not become radicalized and continue to put on pressure. Nothing is less realistic or reasonable or feasible than the utopian dream of winning sex equality within this system.

In fact, the worst trap for serious women, other than reformist illusions, is cynicism about the tremendous potential of their very own sisters to remake the world. Our prospects are as limitless as our spirit and determination.

Women must learn to believe in the power of women.

## FEMINISM: CLASS STRUGGLE OR SEX STRUGGLE

"Radical feminism" is the label adopted by those who view *men*, rather than capitalism, as the enemy of women. Radical feminists decree, contrary to Engels, that women's oppression was an inevitable result of what they describe as our physical inferiority — our smaller size and lesser physical prowess. Women, they say, were historically oppressed by men because men were bigger and stronger and could push women around, and because women, by virtue of their reproductive function, were slaves of their own bodies.

Shulamith Firestone, in *The Dialectic of Sex*,[17] describes in detail the supposed childbirth agonies of women in primitive societies and their constant death and disease due to inferior biology. This variation of Freud's spurious "biology is destiny" dictum holds that the conflicts between men and women are innate, and that male supremacy is and always has been the fundamental problem of human society, surpassing class and race in importance. The quest for dominance is seen by radical feminists as an inevitable male trait, rather than a relatively recent social phenomenon developing out of the economic needs of private property relations.

Equality for women, they contend, is only now possible due to birth control. In their view, we can only be free by abolishing our childbearing function, thus implying that motherhood does, in fact, make us inferior to men.

What is needed, say the radical feminists, is a pitched battle with men, *all* men, over who will run society. The real revolution, to them, is the sex revolution in which women will simply overthrow male control of the system and replace it with — female-run capitalism? They are quiet on this point.

The logical and extreme conclusion of radical feminism is female separatism, which holds that women should entirely sever themselves from men. Radical feminists, particularly the separatists, are sexist, racist and anti-worker in their rejection of alliances with gay men, men of color and male workers. They rely on sexist stereotypes of women as nurturing and intuitive; they trash Marxist theory as "male" and tout personal experience as the highest form of analysis.

Ironically, radical feminists often form unprincipled links with cultural nationalists, who see race or nationality as the primary issue. The sexist and anti-worker positions which are hallmarks of cultural nationalism find parallels in radical feminism. What appear to be strange alliances between racist radical feminists and sexist cultural nationalists actually have a certain logic because they share a basic antagonism toward class analysis and revolutionary solutions.

In their confusion of biology for history and psychology for culture, radical feminists ignore the economic foundations of women's historic exploitation and oppression. They claim that *no* economic system can guarantee equality for women because no economic system can guarantee changes in the attitudes and culture of male chauvinism.

Like liberal leaders, some radical feminist spokespeople have so much hostility toward revolutionary feminism that they have aligned themselves with the right wing, spewing vitriol against the Left and socialist men in particular.

Fortunately, radical feminists and separatists are wrong: wrong in their historical analysis and wrong in their conclusions. Women are and always have been more adaptable and more capable of survival than men. The relationship that developed between childbearing, physical strength and oppression is an *effect* of private property and the evils of an economic system based on it. The key to women's emancipation is given to us by the true history of women in primitive communes where modern value judgments on childbirth and physical size were unheard of and where social worth was determined by women's status in the productive labor force of the society.

This is still the case, and this is why socialism — not reform or separation — is the road to liberation for modern women. Only socialism can once again bring women back into equality in social production and thus to full social, economic and personal equality.

## WOMEN AND SOCIALISM

Women are the majority of the world's population. We constitute not only an absolute majority, but at least half of every ethnic grouping and every class.

We are the majority of the old and the young; we are the majority of the poor. We are the doubly oppressed half of every oppressed minority, as well as the most economically exploited workers. We are potentially the greatest social and political force in the world because we have the least economic, political and social stake in the status quo and the most pressing need for revolutionary social change. The needs and strength of women are the reality that must dictate our tactics.

Capitalism cannot eradicate sexism — or racism or poverty or war or wage exploitation — without killing itself. Recognizing this, oppressed people grope for a socialist solution — a solution that can only come about through revolutionary politics, through a fiercely independent political party of the working class and all the other wretched of the earth.

Feminism — women's rights — is inseparable from socialism. But feminism is not *identical* to socialism. Socialism is a way of reorganizing production, redistributing wealth, and redefining state power in such a manner that the exploiters are expropriated and the workers gain control so that a new era of cultural freedom and human emancipation may flourish on this earth. Feminism, like all struggles for liberation from a specific type of bondage, is a *reason* for socialism, a catalyst to organize for socialism, and a *benefit* of socialism. Socialism is the economic prerequisite for women's emancipation and, at the same time, feminism is decisive to socialism. Where male supremacy functions, there socialism does not, because socialism by definition connotes a higher form of human relations — based on equality — than can possibly exist under capitalism.

The Soviet Union was the first country in which workers, peasants, women and oppressed ethnicities *defeated* capitalism by nationalizing industry and land under workers' control, thereby embarking on the road toward socialism.

In the initial years after the 1917 Russian Revolution, the Bolsheviks made possible enormous advances for women by legalizing abortion and homosexuality, making divorce easier and creating model childcare facilities and collective kitchens. But dire poverty, civil war, and armed invasions by the imperialist world prevented these socialist programs from being implemented by the fledgling workers state and created the conditions for the destruction of the revolution.

Economic devastation and mass starvation fed the growth of a corrupt, privileged bureaucracy which had the power to decide who ate, who got decent housing and education, and who got good jobs.

Joseph Stalin represented the interests of this bureaucracy. He consolidated power by murdering, imprisoning or exiling anyone who opposed the self-serving policies of the new bureaucrats. Stalin's program of "socialism in one country" and "peaceful coexistence with capitalism" derailed revolutions across the globe in order to protect the Soviet rulers. Anti-Semitism, homophobia, and national chauvinism were used in the bureaucracy's interests. Women suffered a vast setback; they were locked into being domestic servants and bearing children for the glory of Stalin's "revolutionary nuclear family."

The historic *resistance* to Stalinism was founded by Leon Trotsky, co-leader with Lenin of the Russian Revolution and a staunch supporter of women's emancipation. Trotsky, who was exiled and eventually murdered by Stalin, spent the last 12 years of his life building an international movement which defended the gains of the Russian Revolution and exposed, opposed and explained the Soviet state's capitulations to imperialism and its wildly zigzagging policies on the domestic and world scene.

Radical Women is part of the movement created by Trotsky to preserve and fight for the socialist ideals of the Russian Revolution. Trotskyism stands for democracy, international socialism, and full human rights. As Trotskyists, we ardently defend all workers states against the hostile onslaught of world capitalism. This is why, for example, we absolutely support the revolutionary people of Cuba in their quest for socialism and the right to self-determination against the U.S. government's bitter enmity and brutal embargo.

Stalinism, and its later variant, Maoism, provided the theoretical underpinning for the workers states of Eastern Europe, China, Cuba, and Vietnam. To varying degrees, these states reflected Stalinist social policies and lack of democracy. But they also brought dramatic improvements in the living conditions and status of women, workers, peasants and national minorities. Russia and Cuba provided the only material support to oppressed people fighting to free themselves from colonial or semi-colonial domination.

Eventually, the constant imperialist barrage and the Soviet people's disillusionment with bureaucratic despots resulted in a political revolution against the Stalinists throughout Eastern Europe. As upheavals rocked the workers states, the world witnessed breathtaking surges toward democracy and genuine socialism. But the working class did not have the leadership it needed to seize power. Pro-capitalist forces succeeded in dismantling the Soviet Union, the world's first workers state, and re-privatizing the economy. The result has been skyrocketing unemployment, homelessness, poverty and repression, with the heaviest burdens falling on women, Jews, and national minorities. Internationally, the collapse of the Soviet state enabled the U.S. government to run amuck, undermining revolts worldwide, invading Panama, Grenada, and Somalia, and making bloody war on Iraq.

In the wake of the dissolution of the Soviet Union, the voices of imperialism trumpet the "death of socialism." But the truth is that socialism has yet to be won anywhere on the planet. Genuine socialism can only exist as an international system. It cannot be born until we break capitalism's chokehold on the global economy, ushering in an era of liberation for women and all of humanity.

## BUILDING FOR A SOCIALIST FEMINIST FUTURE

Initially, primitive communism and feminism interconnected; society was delineated by their integration. Today, feminism exists as a *movement*. Real, undegenerated, international *socialism* exists also as a *movement*. But separation, even a contradiction, prevails between the two movements. Female radicals must strive to remold socialism and feminism into their primal unity, but on a higher historical/cultural level. The inflammatory question, "Which is first?" is just inflammatory — it is not a serious question. Feminism and socialism are related inextricably as strategic parts of the whole. Authentic socialism and principled feminism are consistent, interdependent and harmonious at every point.

Revolutionary feminism demands the direct intervention of women in the class struggle. To sit on the sidelines and preach about the need for social change would be sectarian and self-defeating. Women must use job actions and political organization as a means of gaining reforms necessary for survival. It is only by *our* involvement that the labor, radical, people of color, ethnic minority, and sexual freedom movements can be pressured to come to grips with our issues, which are also *their* issues. In addition, we must work to radicalize the feminist movement and educate women to the multi-issue nature of our struggle, which means teaching them the need to make common cause with the entire working class and with revolutionary politics.

As Trotskyist feminists, we envision and organize for an international socialist feminist society such as exists nowhere in the world today. This task requires that we not only develop a thorough analysis using the sharpest theoretical tools, but that we also are honest, up-front exponents of revolutionary politics.

Stalinism and other opportunist radical currents soft-peddle socialism to gain popularity at the expense of political integrity. But we believe there is no point in hiding our ideology to "bring women along slowly" — as though they were stumbling sheep. We must orient toward socialism *now*, given women's present high level of awareness and intense interest and the simple fact that the *socialist alternative is the only solution which makes sense*. It embodies a goal that is catalytic and momentous enough to mobilize the most serious women and to convey dedication and durability to them. The leadership that comes from such strength and dedication is ultimately capable, in turn, of galvanizing the great masses of oppressed people when they grow ready to move as a whole.

Women don't *need* extended bridges into radical politics. To keep telling us that we need them is not only dishonest, but infantilizing and paralyzing. Such "bridges" become detention centers where forward motion is deliberately prevented.

Women are kept from the fullest understanding of the political implications of our own oppression by a manipulative and elitist political leadership that uses the mass movement for recruiting individuals with "potential." Meanwhile, the movement itself is abandoned to endless activity on an opportunistic treadmill that goes nowhere. Coalitions woven only of lowest-common-denominator threads are cobwebs that dissolve and break. They are an insult to women, even when fomented — innocently or deliberately — by other women.

After years of listening to social engineers obsessed with "bridge building" to the masses, Radical Women can only wonder where all their "new women" are now. Demoralized by the futility they experienced because no one offered them an alternative, many, unfortunately, have dropped out of the movement. They came into the movement radicalized by their experience as women, as lesbians, or as women of color, only to find a political leadership that was unwilling or unable to address itself to that experience with a correspondingly radical perspective.

The initial burst of energy that we all experience when we first gain a feminist consciousness must be tempered with theory and organization to withstand the long and difficult struggle ahead. An opportunist political leadership that does not recognize that *the female experience itself is profoundly radicalizing* holds back the movement by not illuminating the root causes of our oppression, indicating solutions, or offering a strategy that can help achieve full liberation.

The truth is that in women of all ages and colors there lies a vast potential for revolutionary strength and leadership — and at a time in history when strength and leadership are most urgently needed. For women to do less than assume this forefront role on our own behalf, and in our own interests as women, as workers, as people of color, as lesbians, would be to hold back the revolutionary movement and prolong not only our own suffering, but the suffering of oppressed people all over the world.

We are the inheritors of a rich tradition of women fighters and rebels: Ramona Bennett, Daisy Bindi, Tania Bunke, Ding Ling, Vilma Espín, Elizabeth Gurley Flynn, Clara Fraser, Emma Goldman, Fannie Lou Hamer, Lorraine Hansberry, Muriel Heagney, Jiu Jin, Helen Keller, Yuri Kochiyama, Lolita Lebrón, Rosa Luxemburg, Constance Markievicz, Gloria Martin, Eleanor Marx, Janet McCloud, Luisa Moreno, Sylvia Pankhurst, Rosa Parks, Lucy Gonzales Parsons, Nawal El Saadawi, Jessie Street, Emma Tenayuca, Sojourner Truth, Clara Zetkin, and many more.[18] These are women who dedicated their lives to human rights and social progress. They are women who have understood the real meaning of "radical" — change that goes to the *root*.

The future of humanity depends on *our* commitment to carry on that tradition, taking the responsibility for leading the struggle to transform the capitalist system into a socialist democracy for all. Women, socialism, internationalism — these are interconnected in theory and in life.

# PLATFORM

**R**adical Women's platform is the living application of our theory to ever-expanding areas of involvement. Our theory guides our evaluation of new situations as they develop. Intervention in the feminist, people of color, queer, and labor movements constantly tests and proves our socialist feminist analysis and enriches and expands our stands on the issues.

As socialist feminists, we know that the majority of the demands we raise can, at best, be realized only partially or temporarily under capitalism. We strive to win even these incomplete but urgently needed reforms to make it possible for women to struggle and survive. In addition, the fight for reforms is a profoundly radicalizing experience. Women who take up the collective battle for their needs learn how to organize effectively and, at the same time, to see capitalism's inability to provide a solution. Our platform is based on the Trotskyist concept of transitional demands — demands that arise from everyday necessity and cry out for solution, but can never be fully realized under capitalism — and for this reason, they expose the rotting system.

Our platform reflects the wide spectrum of issues that Radical Women has taken up over the years, though it cannot begin to be a complete list of all the stands we take as we intervene in the ever-changing struggles of oppressed people all over the world.

## LEGAL RIGHTS

Throughout most of the world, women are not recognized under the law as equals with men. Current laws and judicial interpretations are sexist. For example, after a century and a half of struggle, the U.S. Constitution still lacks a federal Equal Rights Amendment and thus provides no nationwide legal foundation for women's equality.

The law should protect human life and liberty above private property, but under capitalism the reverse is true. The just and democratic recognition of the rights of women is sacrificed for capital's need to perpetuate the institution of the nuclear family, along with the subordination of wives to their husbands. The resulting second-class status of women is enforced through legislation, the courts and government policy.

### WE DEMAND:

- Unconditional equal treatment under non-sexist law for all women regardless of age, marital status, disability, health, race, sexual orientation, size and weight, immigration status, political ideology, lifestyle, or income level.
- Equal legal recognition of all forms of consenting relationships, marriage and domestic partnerships, including those of lesbians, gays, bisexuals and transgendered people. No preferential tax treatment based on marital status. The unqualified right of married women to keep their own names and independent legal identities. Divorce granted on the grounds of incompatibility and incontestable by either party. Child custody and community property disputes resolved free of charge by a qualified, non-adversarial and publicly funded family commission composed of professionals and lay people acceptable to both parents. Removal of divorce and child custody issues from the adversarial court system. The right of women and children to legal separation from their families.
- Preservation and extension of civil liberties to protect our right to dissent, including freedom of speech, association

and assembly, and the right to privacy in all spheres — particularly on the job, where civil rights are routinely suppressed.

## ECONOMIC EQUALITY

The reentry of women into the world of paid work on every level and on an equal footing with men is the essential lever for achieving social equality. Yet the economic crisis of capitalism deals its heaviest blows to women. Economic dependence, whether on men or on welfare, is in fundamental contradiction to freedom and independence. Women face constant prejudice in financial transactions because of our supposed "emotionalism" and consequent "instability" and also because many women are not paid enough to independently qualify for many economic transactions. To control our lives, we must control our own livelihood.

### WE DEMAND:

- Affirmative action and seniority protection in employment and promotion. Separate seniority lists by race and/or sex in job classifications where women and people of color are underemployed. Legally enforceable quotas to guarantee equal access to all job classifications for women, people of color and ethnic minorities.
- Equal pay for equal or comparable work as a right of women, people of color, disabled, old, young and immigrant workers.
- Free 24-hour, industry- and government-funded, community-controlled childcare centers on or near the job, with educational, recreational and medical facilities for children.
- Paid leave for pregnancy, new baby care and major illness without loss of benefits, seniority or job status.
- Safe working conditions for everyone. Eradication of dangerous work environments that affect disproportionate numbers of women, especially women of color and immi-

PLATFORM

grants. An end to using unsafe conditions as an excuse to exclude women from certain areas of employment. The right of all workers to withdraw their labor, with full pay, from any hazardous work environment or practice until the problem is rectified.

- Unlimited employer-funded sick leave at full pay. Employer-paid, comprehensive health insurance for both full- and part-time workers where healthcare is not yet nationalized. Employer-funded domestic partnership benefits.
- Nationalization of failing industries under workers' control.
- Corporate- and government-sponsored retraining and placement at no loss in pay for injured workers and those laid off by plant closures, automation, or speedup.
- Equal access for women to apprenticeships in the trades. Affirmative action training programs in nontraditional trades. An end to harassment and physical attacks on women in the trades.
- Full employment instituted through a sliding scale of hours with the length of the working day uniformly reduced until there is work for everyone paid at the rate of a full day's union wage.
- Regular, automatic wage increases to fully match increases in the cost of living.

## WOMEN AND UNIONS

Women workers and unionists are key to a revitalized labor movement. As the lowest paid workers, our struggles against discrimination and for our rights bring fresh dynamism to the labor movement.

### WE DEMAND:

- Full equality for women in union membership and leadership functions. The leadership of unions should reflect the membership in terms of race, sex, and languages spoken. Union-sponsored apprenticeship programs with affirmative action hiring and training.

- Aggressive campaigns by unions to organize the traditionally unorganized sectors of labor, which are primarily women and people of color. The labor movement must fight for equality for all workers, address social issues, and prioritize the demands of women, people of color, immigrants, and lesbians and gays.
- Union democracy: the right of union members to decide the goals and priorities of their unions through full discussion and majority vote. Free speech within our unions, including the right of radicals to be heard.
- Militant labor action, including general strikes, in solidarity against government and business attacks on any sector of the labor movement. Solidarity actions with workers of other countries against the union-busting multinationals. Replace protectionist consumer campaigns with "Buy Union" campaigns.
- An anti-capitalist labor party to act as an independent political voice for labor and put an end to the union bureaucracy's perennial alliance with the pro-capitalist parties.
- End AFL-CIO support for the American Institute for Free Labor Development and other CIA fronts which crush independent unions in the Third World.

## BIOLOGICAL SELF-DETERMINATION

Under capitalism, women are considered the property of men, the church and the state. To gain control over our lives, we must take back our minds and bodies.

Our sexuality is for us alone to determine; we must define ourselves. Fundamental to the liberation of women is our right as free individuals to exercise control over our own bodies based on our own judgment, free from economic or social coercion. Bearing and nurturing children is only one part of a woman's life. Children should not be our private responsibility nor should we be forced into childbearing.

PLATFORM

## WE DEMAND:

- No state interference with a woman's reproductive decisions or with her decisions during pregnancy.

- Readily available birth control information and the distribution of free, safe contraceptives to all who request them, regardless of age. Development and promotion of safe, reliable birth control for men as well as women.

- No forced sterilization or "consent" obtained under pressure or in the absence of full information and understanding of consequences. No experiments on women without their knowledge and informed, uncoerced agreement. Stop the reproductive genocide against indigenous and colonized nations, people of color, ethnic minorities, and people with disabilities. Stop "population control" programs used by imperialism to perpetrate genocide in Third World countries.

- Free, safe and accessible abortion on demand for any woman, including women under the age of 18, without notification or approval of parents, the father, or the courts. Legal and medical recognition that a woman's life and livelihood take precedence over a fetus.

- An end to the double standard of sexual morality. The right of married women to extramarital sexual relations free from the atrocious label of "adultery." The right of unmarried women of all sexual orientations to enjoy sexual self-expression and free sex lives, untrammeled by social and religious prejudice and vicious regulatory laws.

- Nationalization of companies that develop new reproductive technology to ensure it will be controlled by and used *for* women, not against us. Reproductive technology should be introduced only after approval by women. Ban profit-making agencies in the surrogate-mother industry. Recognize the rights of surrogate mothers as workers. A surrogate mother should have the same right to change her mind and keep her child as a mother who puts her baby up for adoption.

- Free, quality prenatal care and childbirth services.
- Mandatory non-sexist and non-homophobic sex education for all students of all ages.

## QUALITY HEALTHCARE

We should not be forced to place our mental and physical health in the hands of an insensitive, for-profit medical system that is enriched by our illness. First-rate healthcare is a basic human right.

### WE DEMAND:

- Quality, informative, preventive, and rehabilitative health-care for all at no charge.
- Nationalization of all sectors of the medical industry — including pharmaceuticals, insurance, and home care services — and place them under the control of healthcare workers and users of medical services. Union wages for all healthcare workers.
- The right to free, quality mental health treatment, without pressure to conform to traditional sex roles or heterosexuality. Stop "therapy" aimed at subverting women's rebellion and keeping us in "our place" through harmful drugs, shock treatment and other forms of social control. End the brutalization of women by the psychiatric profession and by racist, sexist psychological testing.
- Comprehensive funding for unbiased research, prevention, and treatment of diseases that affect women and other oppressed people. No exploitive use of women as medical "guinea pigs," which has been especially common with women of color and in Third World nations. An end to the practice of using studies composed solely of white men to develop medical treatments for diseases that affect everyone.
- Full funding for research, treatment, cure and prevention of AIDS. Make all trial drugs free and available to all

P
L
A
T
F
O
R
M

AIDS/HIV-positive patients — including women, who are now routinely excluded from test protocols — on an informed, voluntary basis. Free, voluntary, anonymous HIV testing; no forced testing. No quarantine of AIDS and HIV-positive people. Housing, childcare, medical care, counseling, and a guaranteed income to people with AIDS. Free, culturally appropriate safer sex education and materials for all ages. No discrimination against people with AIDS or HIV.

- Stop the breast cancer epidemic with comprehensive funding for education, research, treatment, cure and prevention. Make all trial drugs free and available. Clean up environmental contributors to cancer. Make state-of-the-art, low-radiation mammography available to all women at no cost. Make all forms of treatment and detection — traditional and nontraditional — available at no cost to breast cancer patients. Breast cancer education for all young women through the schools. Housing, childcare, medical care, counseling, and a guaranteed income for *all* cancer patients.

- Legalize all drugs under community control to take away drug dealers' profits, lower the cost and, therefore, reduce crimes committed to finance drug habits. Allow regulation of drug quality. Provide free, sterile needles and no-cost, stigma-free, accessible, voluntary treatment programs for addicts and alcoholics. Establish universal, culturally aware educational programs to help prevent drug addiction. No forced drug testing.

- The right to make informed decisions about our own healthcare, including the choice of legal guardian, if needed. The right to choose or refuse medical treatment, regardless of pregnancy status. The right to die and the legal right to assisted suicide.

- Full civil rights for people in nursing homes and mental health institutions.

## RIGHTS OF CHILDREN

Within the hierarchy of the nuclear family, children are at the bottom, with no control over their lives, minds or bodies. They receive the harshest blows from the stress, conflict and disintegration of the nuclear family under capitalism, yet have no escape from it. Class society deprives children of their legal, social, economic and political rights through often capricious laws and social mores that take no account of a child's individual and constantly expanding capabilities. Children are the future of humanity, and therefore society as a whole must assume responsibility for the young: to provide for their needs, protect them where they are vulnerable, socialize and educate them, and open the prison door of the nuclear family. Children should be guaranteed freedom from oppressive family relations and their parents should be liberated from the sole and isolated responsibility for child-rearing.

### WE DEMAND:

- The right of children to be respected as capable human beings who can participate in society to the fullest extent of their experience and abilities.
- Free, quality, community-controlled industry- and government-funded childcare centers staffed by professionally trained personnel at union wages and conditions, open 24 hours a day to all children regardless of their social status or the parents' reasons for bringing the children there.
- Guaranteed quality living conditions for children, including full and free access to medical, dental and mental health care, housing, clothing and a nutritious diet. Free breakfast, lunch, and dinner programs for all low-income school children, regardless of immigration status.
- Full protection of children from physical and psychological abuse and sexual coercion, molestation or exploitation by any institution or individual, including parents. Courts and social welfare agencies must make protecting a child from an abusive parent a higher priority than trying to "keep

the family together." End the practice of ignoring or discounting children's testimony about sexual abuse and of scapegoating mothers who are unable to provide sufficient care and protection due to economic or social factors beyond their command. Community control of all agencies charged to act as children's advocates or protectors.

- Recognition of children's right to be sexually active on their own terms and at their own pace.
- Governmental responsibility and allocation of resources at no cost for children with special problems such as AIDS, disabilities, homelessness, and drug or alcohol dependence.
- Implement educational programs to teach parents, teachers and childcare workers how to guide very young children to express themselves through non-sexist play.
- End poverty as a cause for giving children up for adoption. Stop adoption profiteering. Babies shouldn't be brokered.
- The right of young people to organize on their own behalf.
- Stop police harassment and race-profiling of youth.

## EDUCATION

Women are doubly discriminated against in education. First, we are denied equal opportunity in the free choice of fields of academic study as a result of cultural conditioning and closed doors. Second, our own history as a sex is ridiculed and/or ignored in the prevailing curricula.

### WE DEMAND:

- Equal opportunity in all academic fields and in professional, service and industrial training schools. Equal funding for women's and men's sports. An end to race and sex bias in testing. Women and people of color should be represented on all school admissions committees.
- Elimination of stereotyping in educational materials and instruction. Diverse faculty, including women, people of color, and lesbians and gays, at all grade levels. Lesbians, gays, transgendered people, and leftists should have the

right to teach, free of harassment or discrimination.

- Free, quality, multilingual, multicultural education for all, from primary through college levels in an atmosphere of civil liberties and respect for dissidence and nonconformity. An end to the elitist, ivory-tower separation of universities from the communities of oppressed people.
- Access at all educational levels to curricula that represent the full spectrum of human endeavor, including the often omitted areas of creative and performing arts, languages, sex education and the true history of all the exploited and oppressed. End corporate control of curricula and research. The establishment and funding of women's studies, ethnic studies, sexual minority studies, and labor studies departments with teachers qualified to explore and teach the history of oppression and resistance. Required courses in these fields regardless of academic major.
- Expose the cultural-religious myths that claim women's "inferior nature" is scientifically based on biology, sociology, psychology and social anthropology. An international campaign against sexist ideology in the schools.
- Paid living expenses for all students. Free bilingual, multicultural childcare on every campus.
- Accelerated and transitional courses, and waivers on standard entrance qualifications, for women returning to school after years away from it.
- Community/teacher/parent/student control of the schools. Administrators and principals should carry out policies established by the community, not dictate to students and teachers.
- The right to privacy, free speech and association, and the right to organize for teachers and students at all grade levels. Outlaw corporal punishment in the schools.
- Full funding for literacy campaigns in both majority and minority languages. Guarantee every person the right to learn to read and write in the languages of their choice.

Fully paid study leave to acquire these skills.
- Raise the levels of teachers' salaries and school funding through taxing corporations.

## POLITICS

Winning the right to vote was a progressive gain for women, but it has not given us political equality. Capitalist parties court women's votes either by championing the "virtues" of the nuclear family and traditional values, or by presenting themselves as advocates for women's rights and equality. But no capitalist parties can genuinely fight for or achieve full women's rights because they are all dedicated to a system that reaps huge profits from women's inferior status.

Women, people of color, sexual minorities and working people should support only socialist or anti-capitalist labor candidates and build a workingclass party to take independent political action in our own interests. Only such a party will enable us to break the confines of the bourgeois state and create in its stead a new, egalitarian, socialist society.

### WE DEMAND:
- The right to equal participation in political life and all social, political and economic leadership functions.
- The democratic right for all oppressed groups within any organization to form caucuses.
- Responsible action in the interests of their sex by all women legislators.
- Equal access to the ballot, media time, and financial resources for minor parties.

## PEOPLE OF COLOR, NATIONAL/ETHNIC MINORITIES AND INDIGENOUS NATIONS

The same system that oppresses women is responsible for the subjugation of people of color, indigenous people and ethnic minorities. We are all used to make profits for capitalism. The entire movement must learn that we *cannot* achieve meaningful unity by pandering to the most privileged elements of the struggle or by allowing homophobia or anti-Semitism to divide us.

Women of color and national/ethnic minority women experience the most intense forms of oppression because they are discriminated against on three counts — their ethnicity, their sex and their class. Lesbians of color face homophobia as well. They embody and reflect the needs of all oppressed people. No one will achieve true equality until lesbians of color are free and equal.

The leadership role of women of color, indigenous women and national/ethnic minority women is decisive to the coming revolution. They have the most to gain and the least to lose from the destruction of the private property system. It is their seriousness and dedication, born of years of struggle against the racist and sexist ruling class, that will provide the energy and direction towards unity and eventual liberation.

### WE DEMAND:

- An end to all forms of racial and ethnic discrimination: social, legal, political, cultural, linguistic, and economic. Equal participation for everyone in all aspects of society.
- Affirmative action in hiring, promotion and educational opportunities for all people of color and ethnic minorities, particularly women.
- Overturn all immigration laws which limit admission of people of color, discriminate against both undocumented workers and citizens of color, and pit native workers against immigrants — who are actually allies in the fight against the capitalists. Open all borders for free movement internationally.
- An end to both overt and indirect denial of voting rights to people of color, ethnic minorities and immigrants. Mandatory multilingual ballots, voting materials and campaign information.
- Immediate cessation of police brutality and racist harass-

ment, terrorism, and murder of people of color and ethnic minorities. Establish elected, community-controlled police review boards, independent of the police, with power to discipline and fire cops who harass, brutalize and murder people of color, youth, queers, workers and women. The police are the armed agents of the ruling class and are incapable of policing themselves.

- Self-determination for all oppressed and indigenous nations, including Native Americans, Australian Aborigines, Maoris, the Kanaks of New Caledonia, Kurds, Puerto Ricans, and Palestinians.
- An end to racist, anti-immigrant, and anti-Semitic violence and scapegoating.
- End all language discrimination. All state institutions must be fully multilingual.

## SEXUAL MINORITIES

Lesbians, gay men, bisexuals, transgendered people, and transvestites suffer extreme bias because their lives are a direct threat to the "sanctity" of the nuclear family. With the advent of the AIDS crisis, the hysterical scapegoating of gays has triggered a sharp rise in discrimination and violence aimed at all sexual minorities.

All oppressesd people must embrace the demands of sexual minorities for total liberation in order for any of us to gain our freedom. Lesbians face the most intense forms of sexism and lesbians of color have the additional burden of racism. The life experience of surviving a brutally oppressive and hostile society has produced among lesbians a large number of independent, strong and capable women. In these women lies a vast potential for dedicated feminist leadership that can provide strength to the whole movement.

### WE DEMAND:
- An end to the social, political, moral, legal and economic discrimination against lesbians and all sexual minorities.

Enactment of comprehensive legislation to outlaw discrimination against sexual minorities.

- An immediate halt to police harassment, brutality and murder of sexual minorities.
- The right of sexual minorities to care for and raise their children and to be adoptive or foster parents. No discrimination based on sexual orientation, marital status or race against adults who want to adopt children.
- Reversal of immigration laws which refuse entry to sexual minority persons or anyone who has or is suspected of having AIDS.
- An end to the vicious and destructive portrayal of sexual minorities by the media. The image of lesbians as sick, vicious man-haters is consistently used to divide the feminist movement. We denounce such lies and smear tactics.
- Equal access for sexual minorities and independent women to medical benefits, insurance, and paid leave for bereavement and major illnesses. Domestic partner laws that allow all people — gay *and* straight — to claim benefits for all self-defined family relationships. Protect the privacy rights of domestic partners.
- An end to anti-sodomy laws and all other laws that limit consenting sexual practices.

## ELDER WOMEN

The plight of elder women in our society is an intensification of the discrimination and exploitation faced by all women. Self-righteous testimonials about the supposedly revered status of elder women cannot hide the fact that women over 65 are the most impoverished sector of society.

The hard work and poverty endured by young women results only in more poverty and social isolation when they grow old. The inadequate wages of working women yield correspondingly scanty Social Security, medical and retirement benefits, stranding them with increasing healthcare expenses and the ever-rising cost of living.

What little social recognition is given women for their domestic and reproductive services is withdrawn after childbearing age and they are coldly discarded by the rest of society as no longer useful. The cruel poverty and isolation suffered by older women are an insult to all women and a crucial component of our struggle for liberation.

Older women are a very important part of the women's movement. Their years of struggle for survival against unremitting oppression have produced a wisdom invaluable to younger women who are just becoming aware of the harsh reality of women's existence. The feminist movement was built by their hard work and dedication and is strengthened by their continued participation and leadership.

## WE DEMAND:

- A guaranteed pension at livable union wage for all elders.
- Healthcare that is thorough, respectful, and caring. Free, well-staffed, multicultural, multilingual medical and home care. End dehumanizing custodial care for profit. Provision at no cost of all techniques, personal aid devices, exercise and therapy to promote quality of life. Free, accessible transportation. Nutritious, quality meals delivered to the home at no charge.
- The right to a useful and productive life regardless of age. An end to forced retirement and age discrimination in hiring. Jobs and training for elders who don't wish to retire. Seniority rights and health and safety rules to protect the elder worker.
- Free, quality, elder-controlled social and recreational resources.
- An end to violence and threats of violence against older women.
- An end to media stereotyping of elders — and older women in particular — as childlike, useless and dependent. An end to repressive sexual morality toward older women and men.

## YOUNG WOMEN

Young women are doubly oppressed because of their sex and their age. They are prisoners of their families and their education. They are subjected to intense sex-role socialization which limits their abilities, restricts their opportunities and destroys their sense of self-worth. They are denied the basic right to determine the course of their lives. Their sex automatically marks them for oppression, and their youth renders them relatively defenseless against it.

Under capitalism, young women are objects used as their parents/owners see fit. Their struggle against the confines of the nuclear family — and the dynamic leadership they develop as a result — are essential to the liberation of all women.

### WE DEMAND:

- The right of young women to develop physically, intellectually, socially, politically and sexually, free from sexist repression in their families, schools and other social institutions. An immediate halt to the intimidation and institutionalization of young women for their sexual activities and their rejection of the passive "feminine role."
- Establishment of collective homes where young people can live and grow with their peers and compatible adults. Legal recognition of young people's right to enter and leave a family or collective household.
- An end to the super-exploitation of youth as cheap labor. Jobs and training for young people, especially youths of color and young women who are doubly and triply discriminated against in the workplace. Equal wages and union protection for young people who choose to work. No sex-role stereotyping in training or employment opportunities.
- A halt to the exploitation and abuse of young women and children by the advertising and pornography industries.
- The right of young women to make their own reproductive decisions, including the right to abortion, and for social and economic support for teenage mothers. Quality edu-

P
L
A
T
F
O
R
M

cation and childcare for young mothers who wish to continue their schooling.

## DISABLED WOMEN

Disabled people constitute a sizable minority. For example, one-quarter of the U.S. population aged 22 to 64 have some level of physical or mental disability.[19] The three major creators of disabilities — war, unsafe working conditions, and poverty — are directly linked to capitalism. The disabled face discrimination and segregation in all facets of their lives.

Disabled women, in particular, are rendered invisible and socially stigmatized as deformed, helpless, and asexual. Although their sexuality is denied, they are also prime targets of sexual abuse, especially if they are mentally disabled or institutionalized.

Disabled women and men are super-exploited as workers. They are paid far less than other workers or used as free labor. The system forces the disabled into social isolation, thereby reinforcing their second-class status. More money is spent on dependence-oriented programs than on strategies to increase autonomy and self-sufficiency and to allow disabled people to be contributing members of society.

### WE DEMAND:

- Complete integration of the disabled into society, including full legal rights and protection from discrimination. Full government and corporate funding to provide state-of-the-art technological aids to all people with disabilities.
- Make transportation, buildings and all public facilities accessible to disabled people. Free transportation.
- Free, quality, nationalized healthcare.
- Nondiscriminatory job training and employment. Affirmative action quotas for employing people with disabilities. Building and tool modifications for disabled people. Jobs at livable union wages. No exemption from the minimum wage for employers of the disabled. Safe and

healthy working conditions for all. Unionize the sweat-shops where disabled people are often forced to work. Guaranteed income at union wages for all those who are unable to work.

- Equal education for the disabled, including modified facilities where required. Full funding for programs at all educational levels to teach students with learning disabilities.

- An end to social and media stereotypes which emphasize people's disabilities and ignore their abilities.

- Government funding to provide signing for the hearing impaired at all cultural, educational and political events.

- Training on disabled rights issues for those who work with the public. Eliminate government bureaucracy that hinders the disabled from receiving necessary assistance.

## WOMEN AND POVERTY

Limited opportunities have forced many women, especially single mothers, to become dependent upon welfare for their economic survival. This is particularly the case for women of color who, because of racism and sexism, have fewer chances for education and decent paying jobs.

Welfare was fought for and won by the working class to protect its members from the permanent unemployment and poverty that are intrinsic to capitalism. This important gain has been distorted into a system that creates and perpetuates dependency, powerlessness and cynicism, alienating women from the work experiences that build strength and self-sufficiency. If women are ever to achieve equality, they must have training and economic independence.

Instead, even limited welfare benefits are denied to many. In Australia, for example, many single parents are pushed off welfare if suspected of forming a sexual relationship. In the U.S., a rapidly growing number of mothers and homeless people have no welfare benefits to sustain them. The epidemic of extreme poverty and homelessness in advanced capitalist countries is a searing indictment of the system.

P
L
A
T
F
O
R
M

**WE DEMAND:**

- Guaranteed income for all at livable union wage levels.
- Immediate cessation of forced work and "training" programs which use economic intimidation to coerce women to accept undesirable jobs at substandard wages. Such programs use welfare women as a cheap labor pool to break the union movement and produce super-profits for big business.
- Equal access to education and training programs in *all* occupations, not just stereotypical "women's" fields.
- Fair grievance procedures with free legal support for all welfare recipients. An end to spying on welfare recipients.
- Free, 24-hour, quality childcare with transportation and three full daily meals provided to the children.
- Collectivize housework, cooking and child-rearing as *paid* jobs that are societal, not individual, responsibilities. As long as these socially necessary jobs remain the private responsibility of women in the home, the government should pay wages to those doing this work.
- Government subsidized, quality housing for the poor. Stop housing discrimination against welfare recipients. An end to dangerous and dehumanizing "warehousing" of the homeless in shelters. Nutritious food for all.

## WOMEN IN PRISON

Prisons are institutions of social control and inhumane punishment rather than rehabilitation. The accused person's race, sex, sexuality, political ideology and class often have more bearing on convictions and sentences than does evidence of guilt.

Women, in particular, are often incarcerated for "crimes" of economic desperation or for defending themselves against brutal husbands or boyfriends. While imprisoned, women are subjected to degrading living conditions and physical, psychological and sexual harassment.

**WE DEMAND:**

- The right to quality, free legal counsel. Stop racism and sexism in sentencing. Eliminate all forms of discrimination against prisoners and ex-prisoners.
- An end to the racist, anti-workingclass, anti-radical death penalty.
- Freedom for all political prisoners. Shut down special control units that use sensory deprivation and are especially employed against political prisoners.
- The right of prisoners to organize on their own behalf, with protection against retaliation.
- Quality healthcare and decent living conditions in prison. An end to medical experimentation and testing on prisoners. No discriminatory sentencing or treatment of prisoners with AIDS or who are HIV-positive. Free condoms and clean syringes for all prisoners.
- Job training and education while in prison, including training for non-traditional trades. An end to the use of prisoners as super-exploited cheap labor. Employment at union wages for prisoners.
- The right of inmates to retain custody of their children and to choose whether to have their children with them in prison. Adequate facilities for children to stay with their mothers. The right of all prisoners to have unmonitored and unlimited visits from friends, relatives and lovers, regardless of sexual orientation or marital status.
- An end to sexual harassment of all prisoners, lesbians and gay men in particular. An end to racist and sexist violence against prisoners. Stop strip searches and prison rapes.

## LEGALIZATION OF PROSTITUTION

Prostitution is the inevitable corollary of bourgeois monogamy, middleclass morality and Puritanism. Given the establishment's need to maintain the male-dominated, monogamous family — and the taboo on sex outside marriage — prostitution will continue to exist until relationships and moral values are revolutionized.

Again, women are the victims. Lacking job training, skills and education, some women are forced to become prostitutes, a role in which they face overwhelming economic, legal and moral oppression. The illegality of their trade leaves them open to violence from customers, super-exploitation by their parasitic pimp bosses, and constant harassment and abuse by police and courts which treat them as the lowest of criminals.

While we work for an end to capitalism and its merchandising of sex — as prostitution or in any other form — we simultaneously demand protection for maligned and abused sex workers.

### WE DEMAND:

- The immediate and unconditional legalization of prostitution. By "legalization," we mean the complete *decriminalization* of prostitution, so that sex workers are not subject to any form of legal harassment, fines, prosecution or regulation. They should instead be defended under the law from violence and intimidation by pimps, cops and customers. The right of prostitutes to police protection.
- Integration of prostitutes into the working class, with basic labor safeguards and the right to unionize. The right of prostitutes to control their own earnings, free from the parasitism of pimps. A guaranteed minimum wage at union standards for prostitutes.
- Free medical care and checkups for prostitutes as they request them.
- The right of prostitutes to have custody of their children.
- End the causes of prostitution: poverty, racism and sexism. Free job training and placement for women who choose to leave prostitution for another profession.

## VIOLENCE AGAINST WOMEN

As women, we experience violence every day of our lives. Our minds and our bodies are continually subjected to the arbitrary and often ruthless whims of the men who hold power over us — our bosses, husbands, fathers, co-workers, cops, and government officials.

Rape is an extension of male control, a form of terrorism to keep us in our "place." Any woman is fair game to any rapist. When we are raped and protest to the authorities, we are accused of having "asked for it." The insensitive treatment of sexual assault victims by the police, the medical profession, and the courts stems from that same rapist mentality — hidden behind a smoke screen of officialdom and sanctioned by the state.

As an extreme expression of the prevailing "blame-the-victim" attitude, women — especially women of color — who successfully defend themselves against violence are often prosecuted and imprisoned.

Domestic violence has reached epidemic proportions that cut across all class and race lines. Often, police treat marital assault as simply a "spat," leaving a woman undefended against attacks that can escalate to murder. Economics and the judicial system frequently force a battered wife to return to a deadly situation.

The fact is, the patriarchy *depends* upon the violent and inhumane exploitation of women to maintain dominance. We can free ourselves from violence only by joining together, seizing the power, and building a society free of psychological and physical brutality.

**WE DEMAND:**

- The right to live freely without fear of sexual insult or attack. The legal right to self-defense against all forms of sexual violence. No sexual harassment on the job.
- Full police and legal protection for victims of rape and domestic violence. Immediate investigation of all reported crimes against women. Balance the legal assumption that the attacker is innocent until proven guilty with a first priority commitment to protect the victim from further abuse

or injury.

- Prosecution of all rapists with the burden of proof placed in the hands of the authorities, not on the victims. Outlaw marital rape. The right of victims of violent crimes to direct their own legal cases if they so choose.
- Free, sympathetic healthcare for all sexual assault victims. Stop subjecting assault victims to self-righteous moral condemnation from a society that created the problem in the first place.
- State-funded shelters for women fleeing domestic violence. Job training and placement for battered women.
- Compensation of rape/violence survivors for lost income, psychiatric counseling, medical care and any other expenses resulting from an attack.

## THE ENVIRONMENT

Capitalist globalization is destroying the earth. Living under the reign of a class willing to jeopardize our lives and future generations for quick cash, we are bombarded with chemicals in our food, water and air, and poisons at our job sites, in our homes, and in our communities. Women suffer the worst job conditions, and our bodies may also have special susceptibilities to certain environmental poisons.

Women have led the fight against pesticides, toxic and nuclear wastes, deforestation, and other forms of environmental destruction. Technology in the hands of workers can be used for human progress, but under the ruling class it is used against us.

### WE DEMAND:

- Funding and education to preserve and protect the environment and recycle or restore natural resources.
- Open the books of the energy moguls. Nationalize the energy and petrochemical industries under workers' control. Develop safe and abundant energy forms that preserve and improve the global standard of living.

- Immediate shut down of all nuclear plants. Stop the building of nuclear weapons. End dumping of nuclear pollutants and implement community-supervised, safe disposal of existing radioactive waste. Corporations must take full responsibility for re-training and re-employing workers in the nuclear industry.
- Rid the environment and the workplace of murderous pesticides, poisons and hazardous refuse. Full corporate liability for the cost to clean up waste dumps and repair damage to the environment — instead of using workers' tax dollars to clean up the mess.
- An end to all strip mining, especially mining of cancer-causing uranium. An end to the theft of indigenous people's lands for mineral deposits or any other resources.
- Stringently enforced safety and health standards for all workers, particularly those who clean up environmental disasters.
- An end to corporate dumping of garbage and the transfer of hazardous industries to poor communities, Native reservations, and Third World countries. Stringent international standards to stop the industries of imperialist nations from polluting other countries.
- For humane treatment of animals and full protection of endangered species and habitats, including rain forests, tundra and oceans. The survival of animal and plant life is necessary for human progress and should not be pitted against our own well-being.

## MEDIA AND CULTURE

Radio, television, video games, the press, and movies all spew out virulent prejudice against women. Women are portrayed as vacuous, frivolous, inept fools, manipulating seductresses, or simple-minded sex objects who love to be violently abused. We are used to sell anything and everything with our "sex appeal."

Male chauvinism is ingrained in contemporary culture.

Most men accept and live by it automatically, as do many women despite their obvious confusion, frustration and misery. At the same time that sexist stereotypes proliferate, real information about our lives is often censored and kept from us.

**WE DEMAND:**

- End the imposition on the public of sick, distorted and demeaning media images of women and people of color. Cease perpetuating a standard of skinny, slinky white beauty which blatantly discriminates against women of other body types and colors.
- Stop advertisers from using women and children as sexual sales gimmicks. End the practice of employing images of violence against women as attention-grabbers for products. No more advertising aimed at creating consumerist mentality in children and promoting products harmful to their health or their attitudes about others.
- Provide serious media coverage of the struggle for women's rights and the movements of all oppressed people. An end to censorship of our history and information about women's issues. Free media access for all political viewpoints. Programming that reflects the full diversity of human experience and lifestyles, including people of color and sexual minorities. Abolish stereotypical images of all kinds in the media.
- Eliminate the violent exploitation of women and children by the multi-billion dollar international pornography industry.

## THE MILITARY AND THE DRAFT

We oppose a compulsory draft which forces working people to defend imperialism and kill their class sisters and brothers. But we also protest many countries' sexist exclusion of women from the draft.

Women are denied opportunities for military training and suffer sex role stereotyping and economic discrimination in the armed forces. We understand the necessity for women and other oppressed people to learn military skills for our own self-defense.

**WE DEMAND:**

- No draft. Not one human life nor any public funds for imperialist war. Where conscription does exist, no sexist exclusion of women from draft registration or the draft.
- An end to bigotry and job discrimination against women, people of color, sexual minorities, and mothers in the military.
- The right of all military personnel to union wages and to organize unions. Training programs and job placement following military service.
- Free, voluntary military training for all.
- Withdrawal of imperialist troops and advisors around the world. Eliminate the military budget and put the money into social services.
- No United States intervention in other countries. Abolish the U.S.-sponsored School of the Americas which trains rightwing death squads and armies on how to crush democracy and popular revolt. Full support to anti-imperialist struggles and the right of all nations to self-determination.

## THE RIGHT TO SELF-DEFENSE

We support the right of oppressed people everywhere to defend themselves against violence. Whether the danger is posed by rightwing death squads, repressive police, out-of-control husbands, white supremacists, racist thugs, gay bashers, Nazis or police states, we believe organized community self-defense is a matter of survival and common sense.

We do not advocate "turn-the-other-cheek" martyrdom to people of color under racist assault or to anti-Nazi activists attacked by fascist thugs. We do not counsel *campesinos* in Central America to hand over their weapons to the repressive states that have slaughtered so many of their number. We sup-

P
L
A
T
F
O
R
M

port women who defend themselves and their children against rape or assault, sexual minorities who organize defense squads against gay bashers, and workers who protect their picket lines against anti-union scabs.

The question of nonviolence is a tactical issue, not an absolute principle. We do not advocate reckless adventurism or provoke clashes with the cops, Nazis or scabs when there is little to be gained by physical confrontation.

### WE DEMAND:

- Legal recognition of oppressed people's right to self-defense, including community-organized mobilization against police brutality, racist and Nazi assaults, attacks on abortion clinics, queer-bashing, strikebreaking raids, and other forms of repressive violence or terrorism.

## FOR A UNITED FRONT AGAINST THE RIGHT WING AND FASCISM

The economic crisis of capitalism emboldens the conservative right wing and fascists. Their aim is to preserve profits, whatever the cost. To avoid socialist revolution, the system will resort to full-blown fascism, with its genocidal racism, anti-Semitism, sexism and homophobia. Once in power, fascism crushes all unions and workingclass community organizations and obliterates democratic rights for all the oppressed.

The feminist movement is in the forefront of the battle with the ultra-right, particularly over abortion rights. Feminism is the subject of virulent attacks because it challenges the supremacy of the nuclear family. Conversely, women have the capacity to link every targeted movement into a powerful united front against fascism and the right wing.

A united front by definition has a leadership and program that represent the interests of the working class. When petty-bourgeois or bourgeois organizations hold leadership, a united front is undermined and turned into its opposite: an opportunist and class collaborationist "people's front." People's fronts act to preserve the status quo. They always acquiesce to the ruling class — the very class which finances and backs the reactionaries.

A movement to defeat fascism has no place for sectarianism, sexism and bigotry. United fronts must be broad-based organizations that reach beyond the organized Left to also include unions, people of color, Jews, feminists, civil libertarians, and sexual minorities.

### WE DEMAND:

- Democratically run united front organizations in which members are the decision-makers. Each participating organization retains its own program and agrees to work collaboratively on specific actions against the reactionaries.
- No reliance on the police to defend us from fascists. Self-defense against Nazis and the Klan. Confront the fascists in some fashion with specific tactics determined by the relationship of forces and the degree of self-discipline within our ranks. Do not lead people into adventurist, losing battles.
- Solidarity in action against the reactionaries. An injury to one is an injury to all.

P
L
A
T
F
O
R
M

# ORGANIZATIONAL STRUCTURE & PRINCIPLES

●

**R**adical Women is a serious, democratic, and structured organization.

Our internal format is the direct product of our need for solidarity in the face of oppression, our positive program for the liberation of our sex, our belief in the necessity of women's leadership, and our contention that women's liberation is a decisive issue in the general movement for a revolutionary socialist world.

To exist, survive and be taken seriously, the women's movement must serve as a model of the dynamic relationship between the freedom of the individual and the collective function of the group as a whole. This imposes upon us a responsibility for insuring complete democratic rights and disciplined organizational practices within our own movement. We view democracy and structure not as contradictions, but as complementary and interconnected.

A truly democratic organization is one in which the membership is the highest decision-making body. Since alliances of independent and nonconformist individuals rarely achieve unanimity on every issue, the membership asserts its will through the medium of the majority vote to decide upon a unified policy for the group. But vote-taking is meaningless unless there is free, open and intensive discussion of disputed issues. Only when full and open discussion has taken place in a membership meeting can a vote be taken and policy decided.

The minority on any question is entitled to full respect for its views, open-minded consideration of its position, and the right to request reopening of dialogue on an issue when it feels such discussion is necessary and productive for the organization.

Public unity in action is made possible without the violation of individual rights through the medium of a dual-level organizational life: internal and public. Positions are developed through internal discussion and disputed issues are not debated publicly. Minority opinions cannot be presented as the policy of the organization. In public, members must present the majority views of the organization, otherwise Radical Women would be misrepresented and distorted and the majority deprived of its rights. Members, of course, are free to express personal opinions on issues not directly within the scope of Radical Women's program. This policy of unity in action and complete democracy within the organization is called democratic centralism.

Leadership is a necessary and vital part of the democratic process. Radical Women encourages all its members to become leaders. Each member should take personal responsibility to insure that the program is carried out correctly and consistently. Individual examination and analysis of every aspect of the organization, from questions of theory and program to details of administration, provide the basis for real collective leadership.

Mutual aid and group support are our highest ethic. Co-operation and respectful relations are indispensable if we are to project a clear image of our identity and purpose. This tone and approach governs internal discussion, differences, and debates, and can best be characterized as "comradely."

In our work, we aspire to democracy, rationality and objectivity. Sensible discipline is based on mutual respect and ready willingness to experiment, innovate and rethink every aspect of our program and structure. We consider ourselves a developmental movement in the midst of a changing social order,

STRUCTURE

and we intend to combine the necessity of rules with the flexibility to adapt them to a fluid situation. Full democracy in decision-making and full solidarity in taking care of the organization's business — this is our organizational norm and standard.

Radical Women is an autonomous organization of women. Our program calls for women and men to unite in opposing capitalism and building a new world. Our *tactic* for achieving that unity is an independent organization where women can meet separately, build their own and each other's leadership, and connect back with other movements of the oppressed to fight our common enemy from a position of strength. Autonomy is not separatism, which elevates separation to a *principle* and espouses it as a political solution to discrimination.

Because Radical Women and the Freedom Socialist Party agree on the principles of socialist feminism and the need for the leadership of women of color in the revolutionary movement, there is a formal relationship of comradeship and cooperation between the two organizations. Radical Women and the Freedom Socialist Party are affiliated and work together in many areas. We are proud of and defend this alliance. Radical Women appreciates the leadership provided to RW by Freedom Socialist Party members, some of whom were founders of Radical Women.

## BYLAWS

### MEMBERSHIP

General agreement with the theory, program and structure of the organization is the condition of membership. A prospective member requests to join by asking that her name be submitted for a vote to either the full membership at a national/international conference or the membership of the branch to which she is applying.

Each member is expected to actively participate in the organization's work and incorporate her politics into her life.

## LEADERSHIP

The membership elects a leadership that is responsive and accountable to it, replaceable by it, and conferred with sufficient authority to function effectively between membership meetings.

### NATIONAL EXECUTIVE COMMITTEE

The National Executive Committee (NEC), the elected national leadership body of Radical Women, is responsible for providing political guidance and analysis for the direction and development of the organization and each of its branches.

First, the National Executive Committee is responsible for overseeing the implementation of Radical Women conference decisions. Second, the NEC is a policy-making body with the authority between conferences to establish new national policies and develop plans to carry them through.

The National Organizer and other staff are mandated by the NEC to clarify, coordinate, implement and administer policy.

The National Organizer and the National Steering Committee — composed of National Executive Committee members residing in the city of the National Office — are the policy makers between the plenums of the NEC and are responsible to the NEC. Similarly, the National Executive Committee is responsible to the Radical Women membership as a whole.

The National Executive Committee is elected by the membership at national or international conferences. A slate is proposed for discussion, amendment and vote by a nominating committee elected at the conference. Nominating committees are composed primarily of rank-and-file members and include representatives of each Radical Women branch; they should reflect various sectors of the membership, such as age, race, sexuality, and newer and older members. Voting is conducted by secret ballot.

### NATIONAL OFFICERS

**The National Organizer** is responsible for all matters involving national program, policy, administration and organi-

S
T
R
U
C
T
U
R
E

zation between conferences and National Executive Committee meetings. This includes national correspondence, discussion bulletins, national recruiting, assistance to Branch Organizers and at-large members, and all associated functions. The National Organizer chairs National Executive Committee meetings and prepares NEC agendas. She is elected by the membership at conferences.

Depending on the organization's needs and resources, the following duties may be the responsibility of individual coordinators, assigned to the National Organizer, or delegated to National Executive Committee members.

**The Financial Coordinator** is responsible for banking and accounting of national funds; recording and collecting national dues, pledges, donations and other income from the branches; recording and disbursing funds for expenses; preparing monthly reports; and making recommendations to the National Executive Committee, the membership and conferences on the financial status and needs of the organization and how to meet them.

**The Publications Coordinator** is responsible for coordinating the writing and editing of Radical Women documents and working with the National Office on layout, design, reproduction, translation, and national distribution of our documents.

**The Education Coordinator** is responsible for coordinating Radical Women's education program with Branch Organizers, education officers and at-large members; implementing decisions on educational focus by Radical Women conferences and the National Executive Committee; and making educational materials available nationally.

Other standing officers or temporary positions will be developed by the National Executive Committee as needed.

### BRANCH EXECUTIVE COMMITTEES

The Executive Committee of each branch consists of the chief officers and any number of other members, the total size to be determined by the current needs of the organization. Executive Committees should include both seasoned Radical Women leaders and newer, developing, leaders-in-training.

The Executive Committee is the conscious and collective leadership body of the branch. It works out proposals to the membership on local perspectives, policy, tactics, education and actions. Conversely, it considers all proposals referred to it by the membership. The Executive Committee is the responsible body between meetings of the membership and works closely with the Branch Organizer to implement membership decisions.

The Executive Committee is elected by majority vote of the membership. A nominating committee is proposed by the outgoing Executive Committee and voted on by the membership. The nominating committee compiles a slate of Executive Committee candidates. The new slate is proposed to the membership two weeks prior to elections. Written notification of the proposed slate and the elections must be sent to all members one week prior to the election meeting. Additional nominations can be made by the membership. Voting takes place by secret ballot.

### BRANCH OFFICERS

At minimum, a Radical Women branch requires an Organizer. The additional areas of responsibility described below may be the job duty of an individual officer, carried out by the Organizer, or assigned to other members. How different tasks are organized may vary according to the size, resources and specific needs of each branch. Other offices may be created at any time when deemed necessary by the branch membership.

**The Organizer** functions as the chief spokesperson, representative, coordinator and administrator of the organization. Between Executive Committee meetings, she has final authority on administrative and policy questions involved in the work of the other officers. She must approve all activities of a public nature and all matters involving policy that come up between membership and Executive Committee meetings. The Organizer is the responsible individual between meetings of the Executive Committee.

**The Financial Director** is responsible for banking and accounting for the organization's funds; recording and collecting dues, pledges, donations and other income; preparing regular reports on the financial status of the local branch; and regularly submitting the branch's portion of National Radical Women dues to the national Financial Coordinator. She makes proposals for and coordinates local fund drives.

**The Membership Director** informs interested women of the procedures and requirements for joining Radical Women. She is responsible for greeting each new person who comes to a meeting and contacting them afterwards. She maintains a current mailing and phone list of all members and distributes it regularly to the membership. She coordinates local mailings.

**The Public Relations Coordinator** is responsible for coordinating Radical Women's contact with the news media. She writes, reproduces and distributes press releases for meetings and special events, and coordinates or advises on special press releases and press conferences.

**The Special Events Coordinator** initiates proposals for regular public events and works closely with members who are organizing a forum or social event. She provides information, assistance and advice regarding the basics of organizing, and maintains job descriptions and a calendar of upcoming special events.

**The Education Director** is responsible for planning and directing Radical Women's education program. She coordinates educationals for meetings, individual reading programs, study groups, classes and forums as needed, and coordinates the production and distribution of leaflets for these events.

**The Recording Secretary** is responsible for keeping the minutes of membership and Executive Committee meetings. These documents record the agenda, proposals and decisions of the body. The Recording Secretary must maintain the minutes in an orderly and legible fashion; keep them available to the officers and membership; and send copies to other branches and the National Organizer.

**The Liaison to the Freedom Socialist Party Executive** is responsible for communicating with the Radical Women Executive Committee about issues or events being discussed by the FSP Executive Committee and vice versa, so that the two organizations can better coordinate their work.

## SPECIAL POSTS AND COMMITTEES

Special assignments and committees may be established and staffed by the Organizer, the Executive Committee, and/ or the membership. In the first two instances, these appointments must be subsequently approved by the membership.

## TERMS OF OFFICE AND ANNUAL REVIEWS

Terms of office for branch leaders are determined by the membership at annual reviews, which also evaluate the work of the past year and set perspectives for the coming period.

National officers are elected at each conference.

Special workshops, conferences, and other meetings may be scheduled at the discretion of the local or national/international membership on either public or internal subjects.

## FINANCES

Regular and dependable financing is necessary to rationally plan activities, implement decisions, and to publish and disseminate our ideas.

The initiation fee is $5.00, and is paid to the branch that recruits the new member. Dues are $10.00 per month ($5.00 for members with low incomes). Failure to pay dues for three consecutive months constitutes resignation from Radical Women unless hardship arrangements are made with the Financial Director. In addition to dues, members also make monthly pledges to sustain the branch treasury; the amount of the pledge may be negotiated with the Financial Director.

Eighty percent of dues are paid by branches to the National Office. A percentage of pledges, agreed upon by the branch and National Radical Women, is also sent to the National Office.

Special pledges and assessments may be levied for special needs at the discretion of the membership.

## PUBLICATIONS

**Radical Women Position Papers** — Public position papers of Radical Women must be approved by a majority vote of the national membership.

**Internal Bulletin** — The purpose of the internal bulletin is to encourage written exchange of ideas within Radical Women and provide a freewheeling mechanism for the development of new programmatic positions for the organization. The internal bulletin also serves as the chief outlet for pre-conference discussion material to facilitate and stimulate conference deliberations.

All Radical Women members may and should contribute to the bulletin, which will be published in advance of every national conference and as frequently as sufficient material accumulates between conferences, with the goal of publishing at least two bulletins annually.

## CAUCUSES

Radical Women members who are part of any oppressed group have the right to form a caucus to further the aims of the organization.

The Comrades of Color Caucus, composed of all the comrades of color within Radical Women and the Freedom Socialist Party, was first established in Seattle in 1981 after an unprincipled clique attacked Radical Women's position on the vanguard role of women of color and attempted to undermine our affiliation with the Freedom Socialist Party. Local comrades of color took a lead in defeating this clique, and decided afterwards to formalize their new level of leadership and collaboration by forming the caucus.

Since then, the caucus has grown into a national body, the National Comrades of Color Caucus (NCCC), in which comrades of color come together to independently discuss their common issues and develop their leadership skills. The National Comrades of Color Caucus provides leadership to Radical Women and Freedom Socialist Party, particularly on issues related to people of color and fighting racism. It develops policy proposals, spearheads our intervention in the people of color movements and advises our organizations on issues of race in every arena.

### DISCIPLINE

Our effectiveness as an organization working for the liberation of women and a viable feminist movement depends upon our consistent and careful adherence to democracy within our organization and solidarity in the public eye. A member who violates the organization's principles of mutual aid, group support and unity in action constitutes a threat to the morale, seriousness and stability of the organization. Individual members who operate in an arbitrary and disruptive fashion or who misrepresent the policy of the organization will be formally requested to desist from these practices, and the reason for the criticism will be made clear to them. If an individual persists in violations of solidarity, the membership, by a majority vote, has the right to protect the organization by asking her to leave.

### ETHICS AND MUTUAL RESPONSIBILITIES

Radical Women developed out of the belief among women radicals that an injustice to one is an injury to all, and that solidarity in action, backed up by the power of an organization, will affirm our cause to the radical movement and the general public.

This means we owe each other mutual respect, loyalty,

understanding and support in our united and individual confrontations with male supremacy, racism, heterosexism and class oppression on every level of life. This further confers upon us the responsibility to conceive and implement effective and functional tactics of resistance, education and expansion of our roles and rights. Our purpose is not mutual commiseration but to organize around meaningful issues as the basis for advancing the struggle and achieving victory.

## MAKE THE VISION A REALITY

We are confident that armed with socialist feminist theory and a living program, united by shared goals and high ethics of mutual solidarity and collective action, women can take — and indeed *are taking* — the lead in bringing down the oppressive capitalist fortress and building a new, genuinely egalitarian, and free society. *¡Venceremos!*

# NOTES

1    Frederick Engels, *Origin of the Family, Private Property and the State: In Light of the Researches of Lewis H. Morgan* (New York: International Publishers, 1972).

2    Lewis H. Morgan, *Ancient Society* (New York: Henry Holt & Co., 1878).

3    Evelyn Reed, *Women's Evolution: From Matriarchal Clan to Patriarchal Family* (New York: Pathfinder Press, 1974), p. 128.

4    Ibid, p. 127.

5    Engels, p. 120.

6    Ibid, p. 72.

7    Ibid, p. 72.

8    Ibid, p. 232.

9    Ibid, p. 121.

10    Ibid, p. 137.

11    Ibid, p. 137.

12    U.S. Census Bureau, *Statistical Abstract of the United States: 1999* (119th ed.) (Washington, DC, 1999), Chart 72: p. 61; Chart 661: p. 418.

13    Engels, p. 135.

14    Karl Marx, *Capital: A Critique of Political Economy,* Vol. 1: *The Process of Capitalist Production* (Chicago: Charles H. Kerr Co., 1906), p. 536.

15    Engels, p. 137-138.

16    Stepin Fetchit was the stage name of African American vaudeville performer and actor Lincoln Perry (1902-1985). Though he appeared in 49 films, the roles he played epitomized the stereotype of Blacks as shuffling, obsequious simpletons.

17    Shulamith Firestone, *The Dialectic of Sex: The Case for Femi-*

*nist Revolution* (New York: Bantam Books, 1971).

18  *Ramona Bennett* (1938 - ) is an advocate for Native American children. In 1976, as Chair of the Puyallup Tribe, she led an armed, seven-day takeover of Cascadia Juvenile Center which reclaimed the building from the state of Washington.

*Daisy Bindi* (c.1904-1962), an Australian Aborigine, helped lead a landmark 1946 strike of Aboriginal station (ranch) workers. She established an indigenous school and the first Aboriginal cooperative in Western Australia.

*Tania (Haydée Tamara) Bunke* (1933-1967) was a Jewish German-Argentine Communist. Inspired by prospects for revolution throughout Latin America, she joined Che Guevara's guerrilla army, and was killed in an ambush by the Bolivian military.

*Ding Ling* (1904-1986), Chinese revolutionary, novelist, and outspoken critic of sexism. She was imprisoned for her feminism by the Nationalists in the 1930s and by the Stalin-influenced Communists during the Cultural Revolution.

*Vilma Espín* (1930 - ) joined the Cuban liberation struggle as a student in 1952 and served in the Rebel Army which triumphed in 1959. She is president of the Federation of Cuban Women and a leader of the Cuban Communist Party.

*Elizabeth Gurley Flynn* (1890-1964) is celebrated in Joe Hill's song, "The Rebel Girl." A street orator for the Industrial Workers of the World (IWW) and activist for free speech and immigrant workers on both coasts of the U.S., she later joined the U.S. Communist Party.

*Clara Fraser* (1923-1998) was a workingclass, Jewish revolutionary, gifted organizer, and initiator of Marxist feminism in the U.S. She was a visionary theorist and a founder of Radical Women and the Freedom Socialist Party.

*Emma Goldman* (1869-1940), a Russian-Jewish immigrant to the U.S., was a notorious agitator for anarchism, labor, free love, birth control, and homosexual rights.

*Fannie Lou Hamer* (1917-1977) became an inspiring civil rights movement leader at age 47 after losing her livelihood as a sharecropper for trying to vote. She was vice-chair of the

Mississippi Freedom Democratic Party.

*Lorraine Hansberry* (1930-1965), acclaimed African American playwright, essayist and activist, who linked the fight against racism to feminism, gay rights, and revolution. Early member of the pioneering lesbian group, Daughters of Bilitis.

*Muriel Heagney* (1885-1974) pioneered the fight for a living wage for Australian workers, equal pay for women, maternity leave, and union contracts for domestic workers.

*Jiu Jin* (1875-1907) courageously opposed the Manchu dynasty, colonialism, and the subordination of women in both China and Japan. She formed an association of Chinese women revolutionaries and was executed for plotting to overthrow the government.

*Helen Keller* (1880-1968) lost her sight and hearing at 19 months of age, but graduated from college and became a renowned and radical advocate for the disabled, women's suffrage, labor, and the U.S. socialist movement.

*Yuri Kochiyama* (1921 - ), a Japanese American community organizer, was radicalized by her involvement in the Black freedom struggle. An inveterate activist for Asian Americans, political prisoners, Puerto Rican liberation, and socialism.

*Lolita Lebrón* (1919 - ) led an armed assault on the U.S. House of Representatives in 1954 to bring world attention to the colonization of Puerto Rico. Released after 25 years in prison, Lebrón remains a voice for Puerto Rican freedom.

*Rosa Luxemburg* (1871-1919), Polish, Jewish and disabled, was a brilliant Marxist thinker. A founder of the German Communist Party and Spartakist Group, she was assassinated after helping lead a failed insurrection in Germany.

*Constance Markievicz* (1868-1927) was a crusader for Irish freedom and second in command of a military detachment in the 1916 Easter Uprising. As a member of Sinn Féin, she was the first woman elected to British Parliament.

*Gloria Martin* (1919-1995), a feisty and irreverent free spirit, early civil rights activist in St. Louis, Missouri, community organizer, and feminist revolutionary. A founder of Radical Women and guiding light of the Freedom Socialist Party.

*Eleanor Marx* (1855-1898) was a dedicated revolutionary and the youngest child of Karl Marx. Considered one of the best orators in England, she was a writer, strike leader, defender of working women, and major figure in international socialist circles.

*Janet McCloud* (1934 - ), a member of the Tulalip tribe, was a pioneering leader for Pacific Northwest Indian fishing rights and sovereignty, and is an international speaker on issues of indigenous women and Native freedom.

*Luisa Moreno* (1907- 1990?), born in Guatemala, spent three decades as a union organizer and advocate for the rights of Latinos in the United States. She was deported from the U.S. in 1950, and lived in Mexico, Cuba and Guatemala.

*Sylvia Pankhurst* (1882-1960) endured prison and hunger strikes as part of the British suffrage movement. A staunch socialist and opponent of WWI, she spent five months in jail for her "seditious" support for the Russian Revolution.

*Rosa Parks* (1913- ) sparked the Montgomery, Alabama bus boycott and the Black civil rights movement in 1955 by refusing to give a white man her seat on a city bus. She was a seamstress and secretary of the local NAACP.

*Lucy Gonzales Parsons* (1853-1942), a Black and Chicana revolutionary, was a fiery speaker and mobilizer of women, workers, the poor, and people of color. Her husband was one of the Haymarket Martyrs executed by the state of Illinois.

*Nawal El Saadawi* (1931- ), Egyptian physician and militant writer on Arab women, sexuality, religion, and politics. Her books were banished in Egypt and she was imprisoned from 1980-82 for criticizing the government.

*Jessie Street* (1889-1970) scandalized upper-class Australian society by becoming an outspoken feminist, social reformer and Labor Party member. She was a dedicated campaigner for the constitutional rights of Aborigines.

*Emma Tenayuca* (1916-1999) led a strike of 12,000 Chicano pecan shellers in San Antonio, Texas at the age of 22. The following year she became head of the Texas Communist Party.

*Sojourner Truth* (c. 1797-1883), born a slave in New York State, was a powerful lecturer and organizer for abolition, voting rights, economic progress of freed slaves after the Civil War, and the advancement of Black women.

*Clara Zetkin* (1857-1933) initiated International Women's Day as Secretary of the International Bureau of Socialist Women. She was a leftwing leader of the German Social Democratic Party and later of the German Communist Party.

19  U.S. Census Bureau, *Statistical Abstract of the United States: 1999* (119th ed.) (Washington, DC, 1999), Chart 235: p. 151.

# RECOMMENDED READING

●

Alaniz, Yolanda, and Nellie Wong, editors. *Voices of Color*. Seattle: Red Letter Press, 1999.

Cannon, James P. *America's Road to Socialism*. New York: Pioneer Publishers, 1953.

Chambless, Dorothy Mejia. *Race and Sex, 1972: Collision or Comradeship?* Revised Edition. Seattle: Radical Women Publications, 1976.

Deaderick, Sam, and Tamara Turner. *Gay Resistance: The Hidden History*. Revised Edition. Seattle: Red Letter Press, 1997.

Durham, Heidi. *The War on the Disabled: Adding Insult to Injury*. Seattle: Freedom Socialist Publications, 1982.

Durham, Heidi, and Megan Cornish. *Women Workers: Sparkplugs of Labor*. Seattle: Radical Women Publications, 1990.

Durham, Stephen, and Susan Williams. *AIDS Hysteria: A Marxist Analysis*. Seattle: Freedom Socialist Publications, 1986.

Engels, Frederick. *Origin of the Family, Private Property and the State: In Light of the Researches of Lewis H. Morgan*. New York: International Publishers, 1972.

Fraser, Clara. *Revolution, She Wrote*. Seattle: Red Letter Press, 1998. Includes the Radical Women position papers, *Woman as Leader, Response to 'Notes on Leadership,' Which Road to Women's Liberation,* and *The Emancipation of Women*.

Hoddersen, Guerry. *Radical Women in the House of Labor: An Historic Re-entry*. Seattle: Radical Women Publications, 1974.

Kato, Nancy Reiko. *Women of Color: Front-runners for Freedom*. Seattle: Radical Women Publications, 1990.

Lenin, V.I. *The Emancipation of Women*. With an appendix, "Lenin on the Woman Question," by Clara Zetkin. New York:

International Publishers, 1969.

Luxemburg, Rosa. *Reform or Revolution*. New York: Pathfinder Press, 1973.

Martin, Gloria. *Socialist Feminism: The First Decade, 1966-1976*. Seattle: Freedom Socialist Publications, 1986.

*On the Barricades for Abortion Rights: A Selection of Reprints Reflecting Radical Women's Involvement in the Reproductive Rights Movement from 1984-1986*. Seattle: Radical Women Publications, 1986.

Organizer's Report. *A Victory for Socialist Feminism*. Seattle: Freedom Socialist Party Publications, 1969.

Reed, Evelyn. *Women's Evolution: From Matriarchal Clan to Patriarchal Family*. New York: Pathfinder Press, 1974.

Scott, Constance. *How Feminists Can Defeat the Ultra-Right*. Seattle: Radical Women Publications, 1977.

Trotsky, Leon. *Women and the Family*. Second Edition. New York: Pathfinder Press, 1973.

Weiss, Murry, and Robert Crisman. *Permanent Revolution and Women's Emancipation*. Seattle: Freedom Socialist Reprints, 1982.

Williams, Susan. *Lesbianism: A Socialist Feminist Perspective*. Seattle: Radical Women Publications, 1973.

Williams, Susan. *Women's Psychology: Mental Illness as a Social Disease*. Seattle: Radical Women Publications, 1975.

Wong, Nellie, Merle Woo, and Mitsuye Yamada. *Three Asian American Writers Speak Out on Feminism*. Seattle: Radical Women Publications, 1980.

Woo, Merle. *Yellow Woman Speaks: Poetry*. Seattle: Radical Women Publications, 1985.

For prices and ordering information, contact:

**Radical Women Publications,** 5018 Rainier Avenue S., Seattle, WA 98118 • (206)722-6057

**Red Letter Press** and **Freedom Socialist Publications,** 409 Maynard Avenue S., #201, Seattle, WA 98104 • (206)682-0990

## Contact Radical Women —
## work with us, join us!

If you agree with the ideas expressed
in *The Radical Women Manifesto,*
please get in touch! From mass action
to mass mailings, from publication
design to public speaking, from
coalition-building to cooking,
everyone has something to learn,
teach, and contribute as a member
of Radical Women!

Contact the Radical Women National Office
for information about the branch nearest you:

New Valencia Hall, 1908 Mission St.,
San Francisco, CA 94103
Phone: (415)864-1278 • Fax: (415)864-0778
E-mail: rwbayarea@yahoo.com

Other exciting titles from

# ,D LETTER PRESS

## REVOLUTION, SHE WROTE
### by Clara Fraser
Fiery, hilarious, profound, feminist-to-the-bone, and refreshingly optimistic essays and speeches. **$17.95**

## VOICES OF COLOR
### by Yolanda Alaniz and Nellie Wong, Editors
Writer-activists confront racism, sexism and homophobia and explore issues of personal identity and interracial solidarity. **$12.95**

## SOCIALIST FEMINISM: THE FIRST DECADE, 1966-76
### by Gloria Martin
Chronicles the formative years of the Freedom Socialist Party. A practical guide to socialist feminist organizing. **$8.95**

## WOMAN SITTING AT THE MACHINE, THINKING
### Poems by Karen Brodine
"Burningly honest poems."—Denise Levertov. "Multi-dimensional writing...radical in its every impulse."—Roz Spafford. **$8.95**

## GAY RESISTANCE: THE HIDDEN HISTORY
### by Sam Deaderick and Tamara Turner
A lively and impassioned survey of the origins of sexual oppression and the struggle for homosexual freedom. **$7.00**

Order from **RED LETTER PRESS**
409 Maynard Avenue South, Suite 201, Seattle, WA 98104
**For a complete list of publications:**
Phone: (206)682-0990 ● Fax (206)682-8120
E-mail: RedLetterPress@juno.com ● http://www.socialism.com